The Battlefield of Shrewsbury

By

The Reverend Œconomos Stephen Maxfield

2003

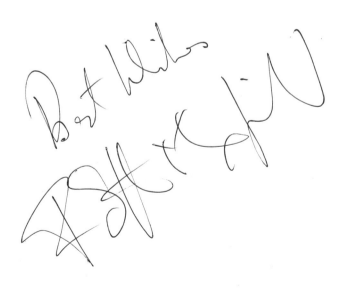

01939 291078

Dedicated to the memory of my ancestors, relations and connections who fought at the Battle of Shrewsbury for Harry Hotspur, amongst whom were:

Sir Robert de Legh, Sir Jenkyn Hanmer, John Kingsley, John Kynaston and John de Legh

Published MMIII

ISBN 0 947805 36 2

Printed by WPG Ltd.
Severn Farm Enterprise Park
Welshpool, Powys SY21 7DF

Cover illustration from a reconstruction of the Battle painted by Andrew Spratt

Contents

Preface   5

Introduction   7

Chapter 1
  The background   11

Chapter 2
  The battle   19

Chapter 3
  The aftermath   33

Chapter 4
  Where was the Battlefield?
  The evidence considered   36

Chapter 5
  Where was the Battlefield?
  Identifying the site   51

Conclusion   55

Maps 1–12   58

Above: Battlefield Church from the college fishponds.

Below: Fishpond to the South of Battlefield Church.

Preface

This year, 2003, we shall be celebrating the 600th anniversary of the battle that was fought between King Henry IV and Harry Hotspur in 1403.

In the greater scheme of things it was not a particularly important battle and its principal interest is that it was the first battle where both sides used longbows. These were used to devastating effect causing very high casualties on either side. It was the battle that brought to an end the 1403 Percy rebellion against King Henry IV. However most of the actual protagonists thought that they were fighting for the King – either Henry IV or Richard II, most not knowing that the latter was already dead.

When the 500th anniversary was celebrated in 1903 a considerable amount of information connected with the battle had been published, or was published by the Shropshire Archaeological Society. There were also a number of lectures celebrating the battle. It comes as some surprise to discover, when reading this material, that there was considerable doubt cast, not only on the course of the battle but the place where it actually took place. In the intervening century opinion has hardened behind a particular course for the battle and a particular site, close to or a little west of Battlefield Church. This short work challenges both views. Very little of what is contained here is new, the vast majority of it having been "in the public domain" for more than a century. I hope however that I will have redressed the balance and re-expressed views held in 1903 and that I have argued convincingly for their adoption.

This is a book about a battlefield. This means that the causes of the battle, the battle itself and the results will be considered where they affect the actual battlefield itself. There is a lot more that can be written about the battle. For instance we know the names of one hundred and eighty or so men who fought for Hotspur by name. A great deal more could be said about them. This I leave to others. There is a great deal that we do not know about the Battle of Shrewsbury; most of it we shall never know. Nevertheless there is much still to be discovered and there are still features on the ground which date from the time of the battle: hedges, tree stumps, paths and fields. In 1903 there were many more things that still existed. In 2003 much of the battlefield has disappeared under concrete: perhaps by 2103 all of it will have disappeared.

I am grateful to the staff at the Shropshire Records and Research for their help in unearthing old documents and books, to my family for enduring five years of cogitation, to the point where the subject has become entirely tedious; to Dennis Onions who read the book and provided useful suggestions, and to Richard Downes, my neighbour, whose family has farmed and still farms the area of the Battle of Shrewsbury and first awakened my interest in the notion that the 'accepted' account was not quite right. I would also particularly like to thank Michael Asser, who not only struggled with my English and improved it greatly but also provided expert information on longbows.

Two scholars from the turn of the nineteenth century must also be mentioned: Dr J.H. Wylie M.A., D.Litt., who had alighted upon what I believe is the right answer, and the Rev'd W.G.D. Fletcher, M.A., F.S.A., who translated a huge number of documents connected with the battle for the Shropshire Archaeological Society and thus provided the raw material for much of this book.

Finally I am most grateful to Andrew Spratt for his permission to use his splendid painting, reconstructing the crucial point in the battle when Hotspur was slain.

It is curious, how many clergymen who have taken an interest in this battle. At least six parish clergy "came out" with Hotspur and actually fought at the battle. Roger Ive, who must have witnessed the battle, was the inspiration behind the founding of the College at Battlefield, the Rev'd W.G.D. Fletcher did indispensable work in collecting and translating documents and I, yet another clergyman, find myself offering an interpretation. The reason for this interest, I leave my readers to discover.

Stephen Maxfield

Introduction

The context for the Battle of Shrewsbury was a rebellion organised by the powerful Percy family of Northumberland[1] in the name of the deposed King, Richard II, against the usurping King, Henry IV. The leader of the rebellion was the Earl of Northumberland's son, Henry Percy known as Harry Hotspur. In July 1403 Hotspur marched south, gathering an army on his way. He arrived at Shrewsbury on 19th or 20th July, at about the same time as the King arrived to hold the town against him. Two days later, a battle was fought somewhere to the north of Shrewsbury.

Virtually all recent books and articles on the battle give the site as somewhere close to the church, built to commemorate the dead, at Battlefield. This was not the unanimous view of those who studied the battle in 1903, and much of the evidence they presented would suggest quite a different site. Nevertheless, the received wisdom of our time is that the battle was fought in the close vicinity of Battlefield Church. This is expressed in several books dealing with English battles but also some other pamphlets and web sites connected with the battle[†]. The general view is that Hotspur took up a position on the ridge to the north of the church, with the King opposite him to the south. The exact positions suggested vary a little, some placing the battle very close to the church indeed, others more to the west. However the church is, in all cases, the centre around which the battle is reckoned to revolve. The principal reason for this is that the church is said to have been built over a large burial pit where many of the slain were buried[2]. Certainly the church was founded as a chantry college staffed by a handful of priests who said masses for the souls of those who were slain. It became known as 'Battlefield' and over the years it was supposed that this was indeed where the battle was fought. There are however important reasons why this site should be questioned.

The first is that if Battlefield Church does indeed cover a burial pit, it does not therefore follow that this was the centre, or even particularly close to the site of the start of the battle.

The second is that the site of a battlefield has to make some military sense and as more becomes known about medieval battles it is increasingly clear that they were a great deal more sophisticated than the charge-and-bash affairs that once was thought[3]. The respective forces needed actually to have been able to arrive at the battlefield, and lines of communications needed to be covered. The site near Battlefield Church does not fulfil these criteria in a very convincing way.

The third is that there is good contemporary documentary evidence, which, far from placing the battle at the site we have been led to believe, places it somewhere entirely different. In fact, it is rather easier to demonstrate that the battle did *not* take place near Battlefield Church than it is to demonstrate where it did take place, but we shall endeavour to make a guess which must be broadly in the right area.

There are other minor reasons which will become apparent as the story unfolds. We must now look at the battle in more detail before identifying a more likely site for the battlefield.

The sources

Something first must be said of how we know about the battle. There are four principal primary sources. The first are the chronicles, of which the most important is the Annales Rich II et Hen IV (1392 - 1406). Most chronicles say very little about the actual battle, and where they do they are generally copying each other. As far as we can tell, none was written by an eyewitness. They were probably compiled by monks from what they were told by witnesses, possibly eye-witnesses after the battle. It is not always certain that the chroniclers understood all that they were told, and they tend to reflect the official view of those who won the battle. They are somewhat frustrating in that details we should like to know are just not mentioned. However that silence may be significant. To be fair to those who were at the battle, one must say that all battles are very confusing for the vast majority of the participants. In the middle ages both sides would have had a fair view of the enemy before the battle, but once battle was joined and an individual was involved in a mêlée he would only be aware of events that were very close to him. This was why banners and standards were so important – they were the only indication as to where one's commander was placed and thus how one's side was faring, advancing or retreating. Whether things were going well or ill at a different point of the line, he would not know until later. Thus the account of a battle from two different witnesses could vary considerably.

The second type of source available to us is a whole range of documents relating to the battle, either concerning the preparations beforehand, or repairing or resolving devastation that the battle had created. These range from pardons, grants of land formerly held by a rebel, the setting up of the chantry at Battlefield and so on. Some tell us exact details of who fought and give useful indications as to the course of the battle. It is from these, for instance, that we know that the battle was first called Husifeld. Some of these records are truly bizarre. We know for instance the exact cost of parboiling Hotspur's head and quarters to arrest decomposition and then the cost of sending them round the kingdom to be exposed above various city gates!

The third kind of source or evidence is topographic: the lie of the land and features that are, or might be, in some way connected to the battle. The most important of these, of course, is the church at Battlefield itself.

Finally, there are archaeological investigations in the area, which may, or more probably may not, tell us something about the battle.

There are also secondary sources, accounts of the battle by modern authors. Here again there is a tendency to depend very heavily on what someone else has written.

---

† For examples of recent works giving this site for the battle see: *Two Men in a Trench,* T.Pollard & N.Oliver; *British Battles,* K. & D. Guest; *The Military Campaigns of the Wars of the Roses,* P.Haigh; *Ordnance Survey Complete Guide to the Battlefields of Britain,* D.Smurthwaite

[1] The Percys held the manor of a small village outside London called Tottenham. Hence the name adopted by the football club representing this village – 'Tottenham Hotspurs'.

[2] The Charters that established the College at Battlefield, could be interpreted in this way, and generally are.

[3] In fact there were a few occasions, at a time earlier to our battle, that commanders **did** organises a battle exactly like a football game! For instance in Spain the sons of King Ferdinand of Leon, Sancho and Alphonso fought two battles by arrangement, one at Llantada (1068) the other at Golpejera (1072). Sancho "the Strong" won both.

Above: Old Riverbed looking west towards the Chester Road.

Below: The Old Riverbed looking east from the Chester Road.

Chapter I

The background

The origins of the rebellion of 1403 go back to the death of Edward III in 1377. The problem was that Edward III lived too long and had too many able and ambitious sons. The latter problem largely brought about a turbulent period in English history that was not resolved until 1487 when the last battle of the Wars of Roses was fought at Stoke, and the majority of Edward's descendants had either died or been put to death. Nearly all those who had survived the wars were subsequently executed by the Tudors. However in 1377 this was all far in the future. Edward III's eldest son, the Black Prince died in 1376 leaving as his heir a ten year old boy, who succeeded to his grandfather's throne as Richard II.

During Richard's minority the country was governed by a regency council, the period was relatively calm. However, when Richard came of age he faced considerable problems from wealthy and powerful magnates, many of whom were his cousins or uncles. One of the ways he attempted to control this situation was by raising a large personal bodyguard of archers from Cheshire, part of his own crown lands.

The wealthiest and most powerful of the magnates was Richard II's uncle, John of Gaunt, Duke of Lancaster, and one time pretender to the throne of Castile and Leon in Spain. John remained loyal to Richard, but he was a very powerful and unloved influence behind the throne. John's son, Henry Bolingbroke, who was approximately the same age as the King, fell foul of his royal cousin, and was banished for ten years and then deprived of his lands. When, in 1399, Richard mounted an expedition to pacify Ireland, Bolingbroke took the opportunity to rebel. He landed in Lincolnshire and then made his way towards Bristol, collecting a large army on the way. Among his earliest supporters was the powerful Percy family from Northumberland.

Richard hurriedly returned from Ireland to find that much of his support had melted away. Eventually, he was captured in Wales, which had remained loyal to him, and forced to abdicate. Bolingbroke was then crowned King as Henry IV in October 1399. Meanwhile, Richard was held in captivity, and after a rebellion in his favour just after Christmas

1399, was moved to the Lancastrian castle at Pontefract. Here he died, very probably of starvation, on the orders of his cousin Henry IV.

Henry was faced with immediate problems of authority. He had deposed an anointed King; he was not in fact Richard's heir, (the Mortimer family had a better claim); and he was believed to have murdered Richard. If this were not enough he was deprived of adequate funds by parliament, so that he was always chronically short of money. The result was a series of rebellions that continued for ten years.

The first serious problem he faced was war with the Scots in 1400, quickly followed by rebellion in Wales led by Owain Glyndwr, a wealthy border landowner with connections to the former princes of Wales. While the Scots were held in check, largely through the Percy family, the rebellion in Wales dragged on for most of the decade. Owain Glyndwr proclaimed himself Prince of Wales. At the height of his power (1404) he controlled not only the area we now think of as Wales, but also substantial parts of north Shropshire, Cheshire, Monmouthshire and Herefordshire. Year after year Henry organised punitive expeditions, which through the guerrilla tactics of the Welsh and atrocious weather, turned into a series of expensive fiascos. However, in July of 1403 Henry faced a serious rebellion from some of his own erstwhile supporters, the Percy family. The immediate reason for the rebellion in 1403 was financial. The Percys were annoyed that Henry IV expected them to keep the peace at their own expense, in the North and in Cheshire, without adequate compensation. They were also unhappy that the King had not ransomed Hotspur's brother-in-law Sir Edmund Mortimer, captured by Owain Glyndwr at the battle of Pilleth.

The opening of the campaign

As far as the Battle of Shrewsbury is concerned, the Percy family was represented, by three men. There was the Earl of Northumberland himself, Henry Percy. He was born in 1342, and was a distinguished military commander under King Edward III. He was created Earl of Northumberland in 1377 after the coronation of Richard II, where he acted as Marshal of England. Apart from fighting the French, he had considerable experience fighting the Scots. He was in command of the army that defeated them at the battle of Homildon Hill (14th September 1402). The second Percy was his younger brother Sir Thomas Percy, Earl of Worcester[†]. Sir Thomas had also been a notable military commander during the time of Edward III and Richard II. He fought with Henry IV's father John of Gaunt in Spain, and after the usurpation of Henry IV was appointed by him as tutor to Henry, Prince of Wales. The third Percy was Sir Henry Percy, nicknamed 'Hotspur'. Hotspur was born 20th May 1364, so he was 39 at the Battle of Shrewsbury. He had extensive experience fighting the Scots and Welsh. He had fought the Earl of Douglas at the battle of Otterburn, where he had been captured. He assisted his father at the battle of Homildon Hill, and had beaten the Scots at the battle of Nesbitt Moor (May 2nd 1402).

It seems that the Percys' plan was for the Earl himself to raise an army in the north and march south. Meanwhile, his son Hotspur was to raise the Welsh Marches, joining with Owain Glyndwr to defeat Prince Henry, who was in nominal command of an army operating against the Welsh in south Wales. The Percy armies would then re-unite to defeat the King.

In certain respects July was a good month to raise an army in the middle ages, but it also had disadvantages. It was the month of the hay harvest, which would provide food to keep the stock alive during the winter, but it was several weeks before the harvest of spring sown crops began. For the poor this meant that virtually everything from the previous year had been eaten, and it could be a time of real famine. It was therefore a good month for recruiting men with little to do, and hungry bellies, and families who were glad to be rid of their hungry men folk for a few weeks to make what food they had go further. The weather was generally good, and rivers low so an army could travel relatively quickly. However the problem for the commander of such an army was that he needed to have substantial quantities of food prepared with which to feed his men. A speedy campaign therefore was essential, before most of the army had to return home to help with the grain harvest.

At the beginning of July 1403, Harry Hotspur with a retinue of about two hundred men, which included some of the Scottish prisoners that he had taken at the battle of Homildon Hill, including the Earl of Douglas, rode south from the Scottish border. They travelled through Northumberland and Lancashire, and reached Chester on "the sixth day of the ides of July" i.e. July 10th. We are told that:

> *"The adherents of the Percys gave public notice in their different districts that Richard (King Richard II) was alive and in their midst, and that it was in his name that they had taken up arms against King Henry; and that if those who desired to see King Richard would appear in arms at the Castle of Chester, they would see him without fail".*[1]

While his army was collecting Hotspur went to Nantwich where he stayed at the home of Petronilla Clerk, who later lost her property for giving him hospitality. "..when Hotspur came to Cheshire, he stayed at the house of Petronilla, the widow of John Clerk, and mother of John Kyngesley"[2].

The army that Hotspur led was very largely composed of Cheshire men, because this area had remained staunchly loyal to the memory of their former King. Richard II had recruited a very substantial bodyguard of highly trained archers, particularly from the east of the County around the area of Macclesfield (Maxfield) Forest. Considerable sums were given to the captains of these archers, and their retainers, both in grants and as salaries. This bodyguard was then used by Richard as a means of oppression, and they attracted a reputation for violence and bad behaviour. Some said that the Cheshire archers were one of the principal reasons for Richard's ultimate fall. When Bolingbroke deposed Richard, the Cheshire men continued in their loyalty, and Henry marched on Chester and invested the city. Most of the Cheshire men then submitted to the new King. The Cheshire bodyguard was disbanded and one of their captains, Peter Legh of Lyme, executed without trial. After Henry had taken Chester he allowed his men to loot the county. The revolt in 1400 attracted Cheshire support. It is not surprising, therefore, that Hotspur saw Cheshire not only as fertile soil for revolt but also as an excellent source of veteran soldiers, most of whom were archers. Most of his army was raised in Cheshire. Over fifty of the more important rebels were from the County, and many are known to have previously served in Richard II's bodyguard, or to have received favours from that King. A number of the rebel leaders also came from Wales, Flintshire, Lancashire, Shropshire, Herefordshire, Northumberland and Yorkshire. At Chester the Earl of Northumberland's brother, Sir Thomas Percy, Earl of Worcester, joined the rebels. Up to this time Worcester had been Prince Henry's tutor, and had been with him in Hereford with the small standing army raised to deal with Owain Glyndwr. Some suggest that he brought a significant proportion of the royal army with him, probably his own personal retainers[3].

The Percy supporters, who wore Richard's emblem of the white hart, gathered at their rendezvous at Sandiway on 17th July. Neither Richard II, nor the Earl of Northumberland with a large army appeared there, as had been promised. In spite of this, many of those at Sandiway joined the Percy army. One chronicler excuses them by saying that they were 'prevailed upon both by promises and by . . threats'. Hotspur and his army then set off for Shrewsbury[4].

The reasons why Hotspur chose to march on Shrewsbury are quite straightforward. Shrewsbury was an important town in the middle ages. It was the centre for the wool trade from Wales, and provided a well fortified base for military operations in the Marches which were being conducted at the time. It would have been a collecting point for supplies and military equipment. If Hotspur secured Shrewsbury, he would be able to supply his army, while denying those supplies to Prince Henry's army further south. By securing Shrewsbury, Hotspur would be in a strong position to dominate the Welsh Marches and co-operate with Owain Glyndwr. However, if Shrewsbury was important to Hotspur, it was equally important to the King. Hence the various armies converged on the town at great speed.

While Hotspur was recruiting in Cheshire, two royal armies were in the field. The King, having decided that he would have to do something to help the Percys, was marching slowly north from London, recruiting an army as he went to fight the Scots. Prince Henry led a small army attempting to suppress the rebellion of Owain Glyndwr. At that time it was operating from a base in Hereford. Defeating this army was one of Hotspur's immediate objectives. To what extent he was aware of the King's forces is difficult to determine. He certainly seems to have been surprised by how speedily it marched.

The King had reached Nottingham about 12th July, where he learned that the Percys had risen against him. He immediately moved towards the trouble, apparently on the advice of the Earl of Dunbar, a Scottish renegade. Marching west to Derby and Tutbury, he arrived at Burton-on-Trent on the 16th July. Here information on the rebellion must have reached him. He summoned Hotspur in order to discuss his grievances. He also told the King's Council what had occurred. From Burton and then from Lichfield on the 17th and 18th July, orders were issued to raise troops as quickly as possible from sixteen different counties to put down the rebellion. By the 19th July the King had reached Stafford. The bulk of the King's army was probably marching via Watling Street to reach Shrewsbury as soon as possible.

On the 20th July Hotspur with his rebel army arrived before the northern gate (Castle Gate) of Shrewsbury and demanded its surrender. Shrewsbury resisted, and it became evident that Prince Henry had arrived with reinforcements for the town. This is probably what Hotspur expected. However, we are also told that the King's banner was flying from the castle, which was a surprise to Hotspur[5]. It is likely that some forces from the King's army had already arrived at the town. Hotspur then took part of his army north-west to the village of Berwick near to the Silver Ford over the Severn. Here he could cross the river and be in

15

a good position to receive reinforcements from all directions, as well as begin the process of investing Shrewsbury for a siege. The rest of his army he left guarding the north of the town.

This piece of country is dominated by a feature called the "Old Riverbed", an ancient oxbow lake which runs in an arc from the Severn west of Shrewsbury and then northwards until it returns back to the Severn only a couple of hundred yards from where it started. In medieval times the reach closest to Shrewsbury was home to a series of fishponds (see Map 1). As a result of housing, road and railway development, the geography of this area is not now obvious. It is an area of marsh or running water, with an escarpment to the north. No army would wish to attack across this ground. For this reason, any army advancing northwards out of Shrewsbury itself, would have been confined to a small tongue of land only a couple of hundred yards across. This is certainly not an area a commander would choose for a battle: in the face of the disciplined veterans of Cheshire it would have been suicidal.

If the King wished to bring Hotspur to battle, he had to find some other way of attacking Hotspur's position. The alternatives were either to march west, cross the Severn at the Silver Ford by Shelton, or go east-north-east, fording the river at Uffington, threatening to outflank Hotspur. (see Map 3). The King chose to do this making camp for the night close to the river.

It is improbable, however, that the whole of the royal army would have been involved in this manoeuvre. It is more likely that some forces would have remained behind to cover the town itself (in case it was stormed in the King's rear), and also to oppose any attempt Hotspur might make to cross the Severn and march south or into Wales. Nevertheless, the King's army crossed the Severn at Uffington and prepared for battle the next day. The King himself spent the night at Haughmond Abbey.

On the evidence of the following account, it is generally assumed that Hotspur spent his last night at Berwick, and that he left in a considerable hurry the following morning:

> *"Finding that he was bound to fight, and that his favourite sword was missing, he asked where it was, and when told that it was at a small farmstead in his rear called Berwick, he turned pale, to the surprise of bystanders, and said with a deep sigh to his servant:"My plough I see is reaching the end of the furrow, for it was told me by a seer, when I was yet in my own country, that I should verily die at Berwick. But, woe to me! The double meaning of the name has beguiled me."*[6]

This 'farmstead' at Berwick[7] was probably the only reasonable shelter for the night close to the Silver Ford, and thus became Hotspur's headquarters. Whether he was in touch with Owain Glyndwr, who was in Carmarthen at this point is unknown. However it is conceivable that some reinforcement reached Hotspur from over this ford[6].

On the morning of St Mary Magdalene's day, July 21st, Hotspur discovered the whereabouts of the Kings army, which was now threatening his lines of communication and his retreat to Chester. In a hurry, he decamped to take up a position where he would give battle. We are told that he chose a broad field, his front protected by a field of peas, which his men wove together to make his position more difficult to attack.

[†] In modern usage when a knight becomes a peer whether through ennoblement or succession he no longer uses the knightly title of 'Sir' but only that of his peerage. This was not the practice in the fifteenth century when both were used or sometimes the knightly degree rather than the peerage. To avoid confusion that might arise in the written sources where, for instance Thomas Percy might be described either as Sir Thomas Percy or as The Earl of Worcester, or even as both, I have adopted the ancient rather than the modern usage.

[1] *Annales Rich II et Henry IV*. Transactions of the Shropshire Archaeological Society (T.S.A.S.) Vol. X 1898 p.295

[2] ibid p 236 ff

[3] That Worcester brought much of Prince Henry's army with him is information that comes for a web site that I cannot now re-access to check. It gave detailed numbers for the troops under Worcester but without any sources mentioned for the claims made. It may, or may not, be correct.

[4] It seems to me probable that there were two rebel columns, one under the Earl of Worcester that set out from Chester, while the other under Hotspur himself, advanced from Sandiway and the Nantwich area. The two columns would have joined forces at Wem and then marched together on Shrewsbury.

[5] *When Henry Percy saw his banner, he was greatly surprised, as he thought that the King had been detained at Burton-on-Trent to await the arrival of his Council. And on that account, having no suspicion at all of the King's approach, he laid siege, in all confidence to Shrewsbury, insolently demanding admission from the townsmen, in order to refresh and revictual his army"* (ibid.).

[6] T.S.A.S. Vol. X 1898 p.300

[7] There are two other references to Berwick in the sources. First there is a local tradition of the Betton family which surrounds a piece of wood which Hotspur placed his hand on for it to be drawn around as a memento of his visit. The tradition as we have it is quite late, but there certainly was a William Betton connected with the battle, and I can see no reason why the tradition should have been recorded earlier. The second is a reference to a burial pit at 'Berwykfeld', about which see below.

Old pollarded oak (perhaps as much as 350 years old) standing in the hedge that was close to the probable centre of Hotspur's position at the start of the battle.

Chapter 2

The battle

The Armies

Before considering the battle itself something must be said about the composition of the two opposing armies, their size and the tactics of the time.

Both armies would have been more or less similar in composition. There were three types of soldier:-

First there were archers, armed with longbows, swords and bucklers (small shields). These were well trained professional or semi-professional soldiers. They were generally noted for their discipline. Most, if not all, would have had some armour and have arrived at the field on horse. They would then have dismounted leaving their horses in the rear and taken up their position. From a military point of view the major significance of the Battle of Shrewsbury is that it was the first time that both armies were equipped with the lethal English longbow. This was the weapon that had destroyed two French armies at Crécy in 1346, at Poitiers in 1356 and a Spanish army at Najera in 1367. It would destroy another French army at Agincourt in 1415.

The English longbow was usually made from slow-growing close grained yew, the best of which was imported from Spain and Italy. The peculiar virtue of yew for the construction of longbows lies in the combination of its yellow sapwood, which possesses great tensile strength and elasticity and from which the back of the bow is formed, and its red heartwood, which resists compression and from which the belly of the bow is formed. Constant practice, enforced by statute, by the adult male population after Mass every Sunday and holy day, laid the groundwork for a potential army of thousands of archers able to bend bows with draw weights of upwards of 100lbs to shoot massed volleys of armour-piercing arrows at distances of up to 300-350 yards. That the English war bow was indeed a formidable weapon, requiring great strength and skill in use, is clear from the evidence of those found in Henry VIII's warship the *Mary Rose*, which sank in 1545. Some of the

Mary Rose bows have been drawn: the heaviest of them required a weight of 185lbs to bring to full draw. The skeletons, presumably of archers, found in areas of the *Mary Rose,* where there are also bows and arrows, are massively boned, with especially highly developed shoulder bones. For such men, trained over many years, the constant use of the war bow would have presented no problem. Even today, archers using replicas of the *Mary Rose* bows weighing 100lbs have been able to shoot 20 arrows a minute. One would expect their medieval forbears to have been able to better this. The battles of the Hundred Year War were won because of the sheer number of these highly trained archers[1], the speed with which they were able to shoot arrows, and their deployment, either in front of dismounted men-at-arms or on the wings shooting into the flanks of an attacking army. *

Second there were the knights and men at arms. These were heavily armoured and also arrived on horseback. By 1403 it was normal for them to fight on foot, though their horses were kept in readiness at the rear for use if necessary. Some knights may also have remained mounted as a mobile reserve. For instance, at the battle of Poitiers the knights had borne most of the battle on foot, until the Black Prince called upon a mounted reserve to charge the last French column. The reason that they fought as infantry was that the horses provided such a great target to archery. John le Bel says the French horses were felled by the English archers at the battle of Crécy and piled up like a litter of piglets. Knights and men-at-arms were armed with swords and bills. At its most developed the bill was a cross between a spiked hammer and a gigantic can-opener. It could be used to smash a helmet, slice the unarmoured back of the knee or prod between the plate armour or through the visor. Medieval battles produced unpleasantly deep wounds from which the victim often died. Once the two sides joined battle, the number of casualties was likely to be approximately equal on either side. However, once one side gave way and started to flee the casualties to that side rose dramatically. As with virtually all set piece battles in history it is during the rout that most casualties occur.

Third there were the less well armed levies. These would also have been armed with bills and protected with padded and leather armour. Their position was not enviable, especially as some of them seem to have been pressed men. The following pardon gives an interesting insight into the problems facing such men, and shows that some claimed to be at the battle unwillingly. (This particular document is also very important for establishing, with complete certainty, the route that at least some of Hotspurs men arrived at the battle i.e. the Chester road).

The King to all his bailifs and faithful men. Know ye that whereas, as we have heard, Joyhn Kynaston, Steward of Richard, Lord Lestraunge, of the Lordship and Hundred of Ellesmere, in the Marches of Wales, and the Vills of Hampton, Culmere and Hampton Wode - lately pressed the tenants - to set out to the same Lord Lestraunge to come with Us, and brought them to a certain place called Mudle (i.e. Myddle) - where the same Lord Lestraunge had not come: and the same tenants - wished to withdraw, but the same John would not allow them, but threatened to behead, draw and hang them. And so the aforesaid John brought the tenants aforesaid, they not knowing the purpose and intent of the same John, unto a place where Henry Percy was, and detained them there with force and arms against their will. We, of our special grace, have pardoned the same tenants - Moreover We have granted to the same tenants their lands, goods and chattels forfeited to Us on the occasion aforesaid.

Signed by the King himself at York on 13th day of August A.D.1403.[2]

How large were the armies at the Battle of Shrewsbury? Estimates vary widely. The highest is that given by the French chronicler Waurin who gives the King's army as 60,000. Such a number is highly improbable. There were no English armies at the time of remotely these numbers (Agincourt was won with an army of about 6,000) and the armies that fought at Shrewsbury were not gathered from throughout the kingdom but from a relatively limited area. The speed with which the armies were assembled and then the speed that they travelled may help to establish their numbers. For instance, it was only ten days from Hotspur arriving at Chester to the day of the battle, while it took nine days for the King to get his men from Nottingham to Shrewsbury, recruiting on the way. We know that Prince Henry was operating against the Welsh with an army of about 4,000, which included garrisons. Some of these will have changed sides and left with the Earl of Worcester. It is unlikely therefore that Prince Henry arrived at Shrewsbury with an army of much more than 2,000. Although the King sent letters summoning reinforcements, only a limited number of men could have heard the news, brought by foot or on horse, and then have come at once. The larger an army, the slower it travels. The King at Shrewsbury probably had an army of between 7,000 and 9,000 men.

If the Percys had been sounding out the Cheshire gentry for a while before the rising, it is reasonable to suppose that, as far as eastern Cheshire was concerned most of the gentry were prepared and rose with their retainers. It is hard to imagine that they numbered much more than 4,000 men. Counting reinforcements from the Earl of Worcester and other gentry from Shropshire and the border counties an army of about 5,000 to 7,000 would seem reasonable. These numbers would be comparable with those of the expedition of Richard II to Ireland in 1399, which seems to have been little more than 7,000. However few levies went with Richard II to Ireland while there were certainly some at Shrewsbury, perhaps considerable numbers. The ratio of men-at-arms to archers gradually increased from the campaigns of Edward I onwards. It is generally reckoned that the ratio was 1:3 in the 14th century rising to 1:5 by the middle of the 15th century. We know something of the numbers brought by individual commanders on Richard II's Irish expedition. They varied from between 1:2 to 1:5. We may conclude that Hotspur would have had a high ration of archers to men-at-arms, probably more than Henry IV. As many of them were lately from Richard II's bodyguard, we may assume that they were well-equipped and trained.

The Battle

The Annales Rich II et Henry IV is the earliest and most coherent account of the Battle of Shrewsbury. Unfortunately, it gives very little of the detail that we should now like to know. Authors seldom record commonplaces: things that were obvious to the chronicler and his original readers may be anything but obvious to us six centuries later. The Chronicle was written as an apology intended to present Henry in a good light. An example of this apologetic purpose is Henry's treatment of the body of Hotspur after the battle. We know from other sources that Henry had the body exhumed, displayed naked by the market cross in Shrewsbury and then beheaded and quartered for display around the kingdom. Many were appalled by this treatment. The Archbishop of York even excommunicated Henry as a result. However the Annales say very little.

> "...because there were many who did not believe in his death (i.e. Hotspur's) he ordered the body to be exhibited and set upright for all to see."[3]

The Annales must therefore be read with caution. There are reasons to believe that Henry did not acquit himself very well at the battle, and, indeed, was close to losing his throne.

In order to try to reconstruct the battle, we shall follow the account in the Annales, then consider other relevant information and so come as best we can to an account of what happened at the Battle of Shrewsbury.

> *"The King viewing the troops drawn up against him with the archers in front, marshalled his own force also with kingly despatch, entrusting one division to the Prince, his heir, and holding the other under his own command. The front rank of the King's division was entrusted to the Earl of Stafford.."*[4]

Medieval armies were generally divided into three divisions, the vanguard, the main battle and the rearguard. When they drew up, the vanguard took the right wing, the main battle the centre, and the rearguard the left wing. Most commentators consider that happened here, with Stafford in command of the right wing, Prince Henry the left and the King himself in the centre. What however can we make of Hotspur's position?

> *"They chose, as it seemed, the more advantageous ground, as the King's army, should it wish to engage, would have to advance across a broad field thickly sown with pease, which they had further twined and looped together so as to hamper an attacking force"*[5].

From this account we can conclude that Hotspur was on the defensive, waiting for Henry to attack, and that the battle took place on cultivated farmland, possibly enclosed by a stock-proof hedge. Before the arrival of the potato, peas were a staple crop in medieval England, providing an important source of protein in the winter. Most of them would have been allowed to dry on the bind, to be harvested and kept for making peas pudding and mixing with other dishes. Old varieties of pea grow quite tall, four to five feet, and are trained up pieces of brushwood to which they cling – little looping and twining would have been necessary. At a number of battles of this time, English archers hammered stakes into the ground in front of them to break up a cavalry charge. Perhaps Hotspur intended the "pease" to have the same effect.. Although it is not certain, it is probable that the King's army would have had to attack uphill. This would certainly have provided an advantage, for Hotspur and for his archers.

23

At the time of the Battle of Shrewsbury archers were generally marshalled on the battlefield in two ways. They were placed amidst the dismounted men-at-arms. At the start of the battle they were in front but once battle was joined they withdrew giving whatever support they could to the rest of the infantry. It could be that they were marshalled on the wings, as at Crécy, Poitiers, and Halidon Hill. In this case the archers would move forward to attack the flanks of the attacking army. There is reason to think that in the French wars the French employed mounted knights on their flanks (as for instance at Agincourt) to clear away these flank archers. These dispositions were not mutually exclusive; indeed they were often used together.

Hotspur had been present at the battle of Homildon Hill†, when a Scots army was shot to pieces by English archers, attacking them first from the front and then moving round to attack them from the left flank. The archery was so devastating that most of the English men at arms had little fighting to do. It would be surprising therefore if Hotspur did not intend to use similar tactics at Shrewsbury. It would not be wrong, to conclude that Hotspur marshalled his men with a mixed arm centre and two wings composed of archers.

The armies being in position, negotiations now took place to arrive at a peaceful outcome without loss of blood. These were conducted by the Abbot of Shrewsbury and the Clerk of the Privy Seal for the King, and the Earl of Worcester for Hotspur. They came to nothing.

> *"A good part of the day having been spent in this interchange or proposals, the King was informed that the rebels were protracting the business solely with a view to strengthen their forces by the arrival of supporters, who were to join them on the following Monday. These negotiations took place on a Sunday"[6].*

In fact the battle took place on a Saturday! Be that as it may, one can well imagine that both sides would be expecting reinforcements from areas where news of the war had only recently arrived. The battle began quite late in the afternoon, so the King's forces not only had the disadvantage of being down-hill, but also had the sun in their eyes. The arrows came 'out of the sun'. If there was the usual prevailing wind blowing at this place, the arrows would have tended to drift to the east, better for the King's left wing but more devastating for his right. It is not clear exactly how the battle started, but:

"the Earle of Dunbarre strongly opposed the grant of any armistice, and advised the King to give the signal for battle, as the enemy refused to consent to what was reasonable. The signal was needless, so eager were both sides for the fray.

On Percy's side as soon as the envoys reached their respective quarters, the archers, the pick of the County of Chester, stoutly opened the attack upon the King's troops, many of whom were struck down, so many in fact, that 4,000 of them turned in flight, thinking that the King was certainly slain."[7]

The *Annales* do not give us the numbers for the King's army, but report that Hotspur had 14,000 'picked men'. If we accept that the King had about the same number this means that about a third of his forces now fled from the field because of the extremely high casualties they were sustaining. This is a momentous statement, and will be considered fully below. In the meantime we must look at what the *Annales* say next.

"The rebel leader, however, and with him the Earl of Douglas, ...aim their attack in mad career at one person, the King, counting him as worth 10,000 others. Laying low all opponents they prosecute their search for the King with couched lances and drawn sword".[8]

All good stirring stuff, ideal for chivalrous readers. It goes on:

"The Earl of Dunbar perceiving their intent, withdrew the King from the original position he took up, that he might not be found there by those who were bent on his death. The advantage of this change of position proved great for the King, as the squire who carried his shield was overthrown by the fierce charge, his banner was hurled down and ripped to shreds, and those who were posted round it slain. Here the Earl of Stafford... and Walter Blond (Blount?), a knight attached to the King, lost their lives"[9].

This account of events makes no sense at all. If large numbers of the Kings men had fled, and if the fighting was so desperate that the King had to be moved, one can only conclude that Hotspur was winning the battle. The rebel leaders, Hotspur, Worcester and the Earl of Douglas were all very experienced soldiers. Why then, should they throw away their advantage by a desperate charge? In fact, the account is not intended to tell us about Hotspur, but to explain the actions of the hero of the story, Henry IV himself. The account is intended to put a chivalrous gloss on a chaotic situation. The King's main battle has collapsed, retainers have been cut down and the King himself has decamped, not to say fled to another part of the field. No wonder this has to be explained by the desperate charge of Hotspur and Douglas. The continuation confirms that something of this order was happening.

> *"Meanwhile the destruction dealt by the arrows, which were flying like a hailstorm from both sides, was very great. The Prince, then fighting his first battle, was shot in the face by an arrow: boy though he was, he did not falter, but with courage beyond his years, disregarding his wounds, cheered on his troops to vengeance. Thus it happened that his division reached the main body of the enemy before the rest, breaking their line, and overthrowing all opponents. Passing right through he faced about, and thus closed them in between his own division and the King. The rebel army fell into a state of great perplexity, not knowing whether they were fighting against the King's party or their own. While they were in this uncertainty Henry Percy was slain, by whose hand it is doubtful, nor were his soldiers aware of it. ...But the King...anxious to prevent the enemy from prolonging the contest in vain hope, and also to check the slaughter, shouted with all his might, 'Henry Percy is dead!' As this shout was passed forward, the most eager of the combatants began to retire, seeing their only hope lay in flight.*
>
> *The King's forces were thus emboldened, and the greater part of the Cheshire knights and squires were slain to the number, it is said of two hundred. Of foot soldiers, grooms and pages there fell very many, of whom we have no reckoning, and Earl Douglas was taken prisoner."*[10]

If this passage is correct, we should conclude that Prince Henry's command on the left wing had not been as devastated as the other parts of the line. It maybe that there was some kind of reserve on the left as well. As a result his command managed to maintain their advance and then broke through Hotspur's line. It seems much more credible that Hotspur died dealing with this threat than dashing about the battlefield.

At this point another rather different account of the battle should be considered. This make much more sense of this phase of the battle, and is indeed supported by other evidence that we have. It was mentioned in his paper, given in 1903, by the eminent scholar, Dr J.H. Wylie. It is worth quoting the piece in full.

> *'Fifty years after the battle was fought we come upon a curious reminiscence of it, which really seems to contain a detailed basis of fact, such as appears in no previous description. It occurs in a novel written by a Frenchman named Jean de Breuil, for the purpose of instructing young beginners in the art of war, and may be freely translated as follows:-*
>
> *"There was once a battle at Cherausbry in England between the King and a knight Sir Thomas (sic) de Percy, and at that battle two very large forces met, and Sir Thomas de Percy broke the battle of the King of England and put it to flight.And then his men all went in pursuit except about 500, who stayed with him and his banners. Now the King of England was not altogether broken up, but still had fully two thousand men staying with him, and when he saw Sir Thomas de Percy so thinly accompanied he marched straight at him, defeated and killed him. So whenever you find yourself in an engagement and you have some men broken up, you should always keep a good number of men together, and don't let all your men pursue, for evil has often come of it."*[11]

Allowing for a somewhat rare spelling of Shrewsbury, and that the Earl of Worcester is put in command of the army rather than Hotspur, I believe that it can be demonstrated that this account is broadly correct. Allowing for the curious passage concerning Hotspur's personal charge, there is nothing in the account of Jean de Breuil that does not broadly agree with the *Annales*. But there is other evidence that gives much more positive support for it. This is to be found in two exceedingly interesting pardons.

> *Pardon to Richard de Croke esq., Collector of 10[ths] and 15[ths], for £26 6s 8d which he owes, because he and his sons were with the King at Salop with the archers, and he and his two sons were wounded, and he lost his horses and harness. Given at Pounfreyt (Pontefract) 16 August (mem10)*[12]

For Adam de lever esquire
The King to all to who &c. greeting. Know ye that since we
have learnt that Adam de lever and his sons together with all
the bowmen with them were in our company and train, and
all our journeys and courses in England, and now lately
were at Salop up to the conclusion of the war, in which two
of his sons were wounded and one of them slain, and the
same Adam lost his horses and harness there; and the
aforesaid Adam is Collector of the 15ths within the
Wapentake of Salford in co. Lancaster, whence he collected
and received £48 9s 8d. We of our special grace and in
consideration of the premises have pardoned the same Adam
the aforesaid £40, notwithstanding that the said 10^{ths} and
15^{ths} are assigned for war. Witness the King at Warsop the 18th
day of August. By the King himself. (mem 11)[13]

These gentlemen were singled out as they were tax farmers responsible for raising the military tax of fifteenths and tenths. These they had collected but failed to pass on to the King, so the King pardoned them because of the loss that they had sustained. There is no reason to suppose that the rest of the King's archers had not suffered on a similar scale, and they tell us that the archers suffered exceedingly badly – out of seven that are mentioned, five were wounded and one was slain. This is a very high rate of casualties.

However even more interesting is the mention of horses and harness. The horses as we have seen would have been at the rear, or with the baggage while harness does not mean *horse* harness, as it would today, but *armour*: hence the expression "died in harness" i.e. died in battle. This evidence implies that Hotspur's forces had reached the horses, and possibly even that the baggage of the royal army was plundered. Whether we should conclude that the armour was with the horses, or with the baggage, or was simply cut from the fallen is not clear. There is further evidence. A certain Harry Parker was pardoned for returning two of the King's knives and seven spoons of gold and silver which he had stolen at the battle[14], and in the grants that were made to a Roger Assent, in recompense of the horses and harness which he also lost at the battle, and to John de Colton and Adam de Aynesworth, who had lost their horses and "the substance of their goods[15]".

This is surely evidence that the King's right wing and centre, at least, were very badly handled by Hotspur's army and that they, along with those forces behind them, turned tail and ran. The bulk of Hotspur's army pursued only stopping to loot the baggage, some making the most of the opportunity to make off on their opponents horses. Although many of the forces under Hotspur, were or had been well trained soldiers, the looting of the enemy's baggage was a problem for virtually all generals up to modern times, as all discipline and cohesion collapsed.‡

The tables were then turned. Had the King held back a reserve? Or had the left wing not been as badly mauled as the rest of the line? Was there a cavalry reserve held back to deal with the archers? Was there a flank attack? These questions cannot now be answered.

Perhaps a little light may come from another source. One of the chronicles; called the *Scotichronicon* because it is of Scottish origin, refer to a 'narrow pass'. Writers on the battle have tended to dismiss this 'narrow pass' or ignored it altogether. However, several of the senior officers on either side were Scottish, and escaped unscathed. It could mean that the battle field was confined by hedges or it could mean that the left wing or reserve had to approach the field via this narrow pass. Such a narrow pass is not to be found in the area around Battlefield Church. We shall return to this below.

If we now accept Jean de Breuil at this point, we can conclude that the remnant of Hotspur's forces were heavily outnumbered and the rest out of control. With Hotspur dead and his forces scattered, we may imagine his troops now being hunted by the victorious forces of the King.

Thus the battle had dissolved into total confusion. Some of the King's men would be arriving at Shrewsbury's Castle Gates with the news that the King had fallen and the day lost, while those of Hotspur's men who realised what had happened would attempt to get away from the field as soon as possible, with groups of men making their way from the field in all directions. That the two armies scattered in various directions is suggested in many of the sources. For instance the Annales says:

> *A more stubborn fight, it is maintained by those who were present, was never known. Very many of the combatants on both sides struggled with such obstinacy that when night came on they did not know which side had won; and they sank down in all directions a chance medley of weary, wounded, bruised, and bleeding men.*[16]

A charter of 1445[17] mentions burials over an area of three miles. If we accept the account of Jean de Breuil this is exactly what we should expect.

An outflanking manoeuvre by the King's left wing would certainly cut Hotspur's retreat on Chester giving his men three alternative directions of flight - either of making their way north-west towards the site of Battlefield Church and Whitchurch, or cutting back and making for the ford at Berwick and safety in Wales, or working round the royal forces via the Baschurch road. Those with the foresight to take the King's horses, or recover their own might escape quite briskly. Those still on foot, however, were faced with pursuit by cavalry and being captured or slaughtered as they ran. Did a group of brave Welshmen make a last stand near Cross Hill, and found their graves in the "Graves Plantation"? Were there others making for their homes in Cheshire who were overtaken near the woods in the vicinity of the eventual site of Battlefield Church?

The subsequent actions of Henry IV, give some indication of what had happened. Why else did he have Hotspur's body degraded and exposed? Surely because Henry had been badly frightened and wanted to stop the rebellion as quickly as possible. Did he execute more rebels than those few we know? Did he massacre prisoners after the battle? His son did after Agincourt - was he following the example of his father?

One final matter must be considered. How many soldiers died at the Battle of Shrewsbury, and how many were wounded? This presents a problem as the figures of the numbers dead and wounded vary very widely, from a maximum of 16,000 dead, to a minimum of 1,600. Presumably the former is a miscopying of the latter. However, sometimes the figures for the number buried in a pit are very precise - 1,847 and 2,291. Given that there were at least two and perhaps more burial pits, this divergence is not so surprising. It should be remembered that some of the slain will have been collected by their families and buried at home, and that a considerable number of those who were wounded and made off from the battlefield died later, from tetanus, gangrene and septicaemia.

Perhaps we should approach the question from a different angle. It was highly unusual in any open battle before the First World War for an army to lose more than 25% of its effectives. Consideration of a medieval battle will explain why this was so. The two sides would be lined up opposite each other when the battle began. If they faced punishing archery, they would come to grips as soon as possible. As men were killed or wounded gaps would form in the line, and these would be filled from the back ranks. For this reason medieval armies would be drawn up in many ranks: Lt Col. A. Burne suggests that at the Battle of Shrewsbury there would have been at least eight.[18] Of course not all those who were wounded would drop where they fell; most would attempt to get back through the ranks away to safety. Sometimes they would be helped by their colleagues, creating even greater gaps. Thus as the fight continued there would be a steady drift of troops away from the battle. Sooner or later one side or the other would be affected by this drift to the point that the holding of the line would become untenable. Unless the line was reinforced by reserves, it would break. From this moment, slaughter on a larger scale would begin. Along much of the line the troops would hold and would retire in reasonable order. Inevitably like water the victorious force would flow to the point of least resistance.

If the Battle of Shrewsbury was indeed exceptionally bloody as the chroniclers claim we can assume that 25% of the effectives were casualties. If we then allow for a total figure for combatants of around 12,000, we may conclude about 3,000 casualties in total of whom a high proportion would die. Therefore a figure of 2,000 for the number of dead seems about right. There is a curious feature however, about the Battle of Shrewsbury, which again bears out the account of Jean de Breuil. It seems that the victors sustained higher casualties than the losers. For instance we know from one chronicle of the names of sixteen knights who fought for the King who died as opposed to eight who fought for Hotspur. Other chronicles confirm this ratio. These figures suggest that the King's men fared very badly when their line collapsed, but that after the change in fortunes of the battle many of Hotspur's men made good their escape.

*The main tactical problem in the late medieval period was how to deal with a charge by heavy cavalry which literally swept all before it. Various things were tried. The Scots for instance used a formation of spearmen which was quite successful. The English used a combination of massed archers and heavy infantry. This was a spectacularly successful solution which was tried until armour became more sophisticated and proof against arrows, and ways were found, such as opposing archers and artillery to deal with the English bowmen. It is mistaken to think that Crécy was the first time that this tactic was used. It was, for instance, used to good effect at the much earlier battle of Bourgthéroulde in 1124.

† Lest there be some confusion it should be known that there were two battles when the English fought the Scots at places with similar sounding names. The battle of Halidon Hill was fought on July 19th 1333, while the battle of Homildon Hill was fought 14th September 1402.

‡ Not such an ancient problem either. I recall the relish in my father's voice when talking about certain aspects of the D-Day landings in which he took part. His unit of the Royal Marines were one of the first to land and took over the German commandants headquarters. The cellar was found to be full of pink champagne..!

1 See *The Medieval Archer* by Jim Bradbury on this point.

[2] T.S.A.S. Vol. X 1898 p227ff. I am very grateful to Mr Christopher Jobson for bringing my attention to this most important document. [3] T.S.A.S. Vol. X p 305 [4] ibid. p. 302 [5] ibid p. 301 [6] ibid. p. 302 [7] ibid. [8] ibid. [9] ibid. [10] ibid. and 303.

[11] *Five Hundred Years Ago* by J.H.Wylie T.S.A.S. Series 3 Vol. 3 1903 p.142.

[12] T.S.A.S. Vol. X 1898 p.240 [13] ibid. p.241 [14] ibid. p.238 [15] ibid p.240 [16] ibid p.240 [17] *The Battle of Shrewsbury 1403*, E.J.Priestley p.14 [18] *The Battle of Shrewsbury: a military reconstruction* T.S.A.S. Vol. 52

Albright Hussey today: now an hotel and restaurant.

Chapter 3

The aftermath

As the sun went down on that July day, new activity began. The victors along with the good peasants of Albrighton, Harlescott, and doubtless Shrewsbury itself, started plundering and stripping the dead and wounded. Everything was valuable, money, clothes, leather, weapons and armour. This process would probably have gone on for weeks. We have an account of exactly what it might entail:-

"Sir R. Gousile, who had received knighthood that day.. was not killed in battle, but by the treachery of his own servant, when he had left the fight wounded in the side. He was lying under a hedge seemingly at his last gasp, when one of his household (a special favourite) came up. This man had run away at the beginning of the fighting, and when it was over had come back, like a grave robber, after the manner of such folk, to plunder the bodies of the slain. He came down alone as it happened, to the place where his master was lying, and recognised him by the badges on his armour. Being himself recognised by his master, he asked him how he fared, "I am alive," he answered with difficulty: "But nearly stifled by my armour, take off my gauntlets and coat armour, if haply I may so be restored to life." When his hands were set free, he gave the servant a ring to take to his wife, and told him that there were sixty marks in his purse. This money he bid the man to keep safe for his master's sustenance, should he live, but should he die, then to take it for his own use.

But what of the treacherous villain who had already forsaken his master? Arrant coward in the battle, he bared his master's heaving breast as he lay, and there ran him through, still thrusting the steel into the quivering body, til he saw him quite dead. This done, he laid hands on collar, jewels, rings, and other badges of his rank, as well as the money above mentioned, leaving under the hedge the stripped corpse of his

*master. All this was seen and heard by an esquire, who had
also quitted the battle, and, himself wounded and overborne
by the weight of his armour, had crawled on hands and
knees to the same hedge for the sake of the cool breeze. He
afterwards recovered, and made known the crime of the
scoundrel, telling the whole story to his mistress, the Duchess
of Norfolk. The murderer, subsequently convicted by the
evidence of the stolen goods, was punished as he deserved.*

The King allowed the bodies to be buried the following day. Hotspur's
body was given to his kinsmen to bury, and it is suggested that it was buried
at Whitchurch. This seems unlikely, given the distance and the time
available. On Monday the King repented of this decision, and had Hotspur's
body exhumed and brought to Shrewsbury and exposed naked by the cross
at the top of Pride Hill, propped between two millstones. These seem
curious implements for attaching anything. Perhaps the two millstones
provided a base for a stake placed between them both to which the body
was attached. On the same day a number of the rebels were hanged drawn
and quartered. These included Thomas Percy, Earl of Worcester, Richard
Venables, Baron Kinderton, Richard Le Vernon, Baron Shybrook, and one
chronicle says "and many others". Probably many ordinary soldiers were
put to death. This would have had considerable impact on a border town
like Shrewsbury, and may perhaps have motivated Roger Ive and Richard
Hussey to found the College at Battlefield.

Some recent authors have been wary of accepting that any of these
rebels were actually hanged drawn and quartered, stating only that they
were beheaded. There can be no doubt that the rebels met the normal
penalty for treason, which remained the English custom right down to
1715[1], of hanging, drawing and quartering. The body of Hotspur was
also beheaded and quartered the fragments being distributed for
exposition round the country.

It is surprising that Henry IV considered it necessary to expose
Hotspur's corpse. His exhumation was considered very appalling at the
time and Henry was even excommunicated by the Archbishop of York for
the act. It seems that the King had had a very considerable fright, and
had come remarkably close to losing his throne.

Many rebels had their property seized. This situation lasted for only a
matter of months' after which there was a general amnesty and most,
including the Earl of Northumberland, were pardoned and recovered
their property. The maintenance of order in Cheshire may have been the
reason for the amnesty.

[1] This was the fate of those executed after the Jacobite rising of 1715 at Tyburn and elsewhere. "The victim was dragged on a hurdle, pulled by a horse. He was then hung on a gibbet like the lowest form of thief, but taken down before actually dead. Revived and brought to consciousness with cold water, he was laid on a table and had his stomach cut open. His intestines having been pulled out and burnt his body was hacked into quarters, which were later stuck up in suitable places to warn others of the danger of treason. The whole process was watched by huge crowds. At what stage the wretched victim actually died probably depended on the size of tip given to the public hangman; no doubt the latter could speed up death or prolong life as he saw fit". *The Jacobite Rising of 1715,* John Baynes p189

The Graves, looking east from the Shrewsbury to Chester railway over Big Graves towards Little Graves now planted with trees.

Chapter 4

Where was the battlefield?
The evidence considered

First it is necessary to establish what actually is meant by the "battlefield". I take this to mean the place where the two armies were first drawn up and where the battle began. Not all the fighting took place here. There would have been fighting during the pursuit of the King's forces by Hotspur's, and then the pursuit of Hotspur's forces as they endeavoured to leave the field. An area from Berwick to Albrighton to Battlefield Church and down to Shrewsbury itself could have seen some fighting - much of it fierce.

In order to locate the battlefield the following needs to be considered:
1) fixed features in the landscape that are definitely, or might be connected with the battle, and local oral traditions connected with them;
2) documentary evidence, both written and maps;
3) archaeology.

Features in the Landscape

Battlefield Church
The first and most significant is the church at Battlefield itself.

The church was built in 1409 for a chantry college founded by the parish priest of Albright Hussey and Fitz, Roger Ive. It seems that the idea for the chantry was his and he was given two acres of land, called Hateley Field, by Richard Hussey, of Albright Hussey for the purpose. He applied to the King for permission to give the land, which was granted, along with various means of income for the supporting the college. These included the advowsons of Michaelskirk in Lancashire and the chapel in Shrewsbury castle, which also included St Juliana's church. The King also gave Roger Ive seven fodders of lead for the roof. For some reason which is not altogether clear Roger Ive surrendered the land and foundation to the King in 1410, who promptly assigned it back to him. The original intention was for the college to consist of eight chaplains, of whom one should be the master. In fact this number was never achieved, and the college was established with six chaplains, one of whom was the master.

The purpose of a chantry was to offer prayers, and particularly the Mass for the souls of the dead. That prayers should be offered for the dead was never an issue in Christianity for the first 1,500 years of its existence. This was partly because praying for the dead is commended in the Old Testament (Macc:12:44-5), partly because it was always a practice for Christians (some of the very earliest prayers that we have in the catacombs are of this nature). In western Christendom after the 11th century these prayers became more elaborate, due to the emphasis on the doctrine of purgatory. This is thought of as a place where souls are transported after death, where they suffer the consequence of the sins committed in this life. It was and is believed that prayers offered for souls in purgatory hastened their journey. As a result a large number of special chapels called chantries were established for this purpose, often actually inside other churches such as cathedrals, large parish churches and monasteries. These generally took the form of small chapels within the church, usually close to the tomb of the beneficiary. Many of these chapels still exist and are a delightful feature of English cathedrals. As a rule, there was a single chaplain responsible for saying the chantry mass every day for the founder or founders of the chantry. The grant establishing the chantry seldom remained adequate for the maintenance of the priest, so many of these priests had other occupations as well, often as school masters. This was the case at Battlefield, where a school was established. For instance in 1581 John Clarke, then aged 64, spoke of having been to school there 55 years before, i.e. in 1528. The chantries, along with the schools that they provided, were swept away in 1547 during the Protestant Reformation, in Edward VI's reign.

However, the chantry at Battlefield was unique. In no other battlefield in England was a chantry established to pray for those who fell in the battle, let alone a college with six chaplains! Indeed, the establishment of a chantry college was a rare thing.

We are fortunate in still having the will of Roger Ive dating from 1444 (he died in 1447); in which he lays down detailed rules for the chaplains. They were required to say a Mass every day as well as Matins and Vespers for the dead. They had to eat the two meals of the day (dinner and supper) together in the college, and they were not allowed to leave the college without the permission of the master on pain of a fine of 3s 4d. For their services they were paid ten marks a year. Out of this they had to pay four marks for their board and lodging. A mark was worth 13s 4d on the basis of 20 silver pennies to an ounce.

The services in the college were served with considerable ceremony. For example, Roger Ive left six sets of vestments to the college including two high mass sets, in red and white, with chasuble, cope, and two dalmatics. He also left several chalice sets and a magnificent collection of service books for the worship, much of which was required to be conducted "with note" i.e. sung.

The establishment of the college at Battlefield raises three questions:-

1) Was this the place where the battle was fought?
2) Was this the place that the fallen were buried?
3) Why was this unique institution founded after this, relatively unimportant, battle?

Was this the place where the battle was fought?

It has to be said, first of all, that the overwhelming majority of authors and scholars writing about the battle have believed that it was, and those who have been less certain have been reluctant to suggest any alternative site. The reason for believing that it was, indeed, the site of the battle depends to a great extent, though not exclusively, on the wording of the charters used to found the college. Here is an example:

> "...we have granted and given license for us and our heirs, so far as in us lies, to our beloved Richard Huse esquire that he can give and assign to our beloved Roger Yve (Ive) chaplain and John Gilberd chaplain, two acres of land with the appurtenances in Adbrighton Huse in the County of Salop, **lying in a certain field called Hateleyfeld in which there was a battle** between us and Henry Percy lately our adversary deceased..."[1] (emphasis mine)

All the initial charters[2] referring to the establishment and life of the college are expressed in the same terms. On the face of it they seem pretty conclusive: the battle took place in Hateleyfeld, where the college is sited. This has convinced most of those writing about the battle. But is this a reasonable way to read these charters? For instance does the clause "in which there was a battle" refer to Hateleyfeld or does it rather refer to Adbright Hussey a much larger area altogether? Can we really believe that the clerks or originators of these charters believed that a battle between at the least several thousand men could take place in a two acre field? Surely these phrases and clauses at the beginning of the charters were intended to identify the site with a broad reason for its purpose, not the exact location of the battle?

There is other evidence. When the site of the *battle* itself is being located, (as opposed to the *college*), in pardons and other such documents, it is never placed in Hateleyfeld, but always somewhere else. Indeed, Hateleyfeld is not mentioned. This point will be discussed more fully below, when considering the documentary evidence for the site of the *battle*, rather than the *college*. We must, I believe, seriously question and doubt that the evidence from the charters establishing the college gives us the site of the battle itself.

Was this the place that the fallen were buried?

Much of what has been written about the Battle of Shrewsbury mentions that the slain were buried near or under Battlefield Church. This provided the rationale for the *'Two Men in Trench'* television programme (2002), where an excavation of part of the churchyard was undertaken. No grave was found. The implication behind this is that the slain are buried close to where they fall, and therefore this is evidence for the location of a battle. In fact the slain are *not* necessarily buried where they fall, nor is the place that they fall *necessarily* a guide to the location of the battlefield.

Burial pits are features of many battlefields, because it is much more efficient to bury dead bodies in pits or large holes than in individual graves. Where these pits come to be dug is dependant on a number of factors, like soil, gravity (dead bodies are easier to drag downhill than up), the availability of carts, and the wishes of the landowner, who will not want good ground or the middle of his fields excavated.

It does *not* therefore follow that a burial pit can be used as a guide to the location of a battlefield. Sometimes burial pits were dug quite a distance away. An example of this is the two burial pits dug after the battle of Towton in 1461. These are sited by a farm near the 'Crooked Billet' public house, a good mile and a half from the centre of the battle.

As already mentioned, the area of fiercest fighting is not necessarily where the majority of the casualties are sustained. These occur when the defeated army retreats or flees, turning their backs on the enemy.

However, there is quite a lot of circumstantial evidence that at least some of the fallen were buried near Battlefield College, not least by the foundation charters of the college. But this matter has been greatly obfuscated by one of the chroniclers who says:

> *"... The Battle of Salop or Schroobisberry in the field called baitlefeld otherwise Berwykfeld near Salop ... where were slain of chiefs 2,291 entombed in a pit in length 160 feet, breadth 68 feet and in depth 60 feet..."*[3]

39

This is an enormous hole! If dug on the site of Battlefield Church it would have filled with water long before 60 feet was reached and would have taken a huge labour force in the digging. It would have provided the worst imaginable foundation for a church which has stood very satisfactorily for 600 years. The writer of this manuscript was exact about the number who were fallen; he may have been equally so in his mathematics and worked out the size of hole necessary for this number of bodies using some unknown formula.

The reference to 'Berwykfeld' in this account is curious. As we have seen there are other connections with Berwick. Does this grave pit refer to the area near to Berwick called Graves Plantation? (see below), which could well be so described and not to Battlefield at all?

This does not mean that Battlefield Church is *not* the site of a grave pit. It is a very large church and may well cover a substantial grave pit, or there may be one somewhere in the graveyard. But neither does it mean that it is the site of the battle.

Fish
Before leaving the subject of Battlefield Church we must consider if there were any factors which commended the site as suitable for a college foundation apart from its proximity to the battlefield. There is certainly one factor, unmentioned in the literature on the battle, so obvious would it have been to the medieval mind, that has a considerable bearing on the siting of the college: a supply of fresh fish. Medieval western Christians were required to fast and abstain from meat on every Wednesday and Friday and all through Lent. Fresh fish, particularly in an inland county like Shropshire was in short supply and expensive. It is inconceivable that any religious foundation would have been built without consideration of this discipline. Either the house had to have access to a river or the sea or it had to be located in a place where good fish ponds could be dug, supplied with water and carp reared. Battlefield Church is in precisely such a site, the carp ponds are still in existence and even now after 600 years they could, with only a little effort, be brought back into production. It is possible that Roger Ive requested this land from Richard Hussey because of its potential as a fishery, as well as its proximity to the battlefield.

Other features in the landscape

All the features (see Map 4) considered at this point are places which tradition, in one way or another, connects with the Battle of Shrewsbury.

It is important that they are considered with caution. They *might* be significant, but they might not, and indeed, the original significance may now be entirely forgotten.

Graves Plantation

Three-quarters of a mile almost due west of the cross roads at Harlescott is a piece of woodland marked on the Ordnance survey maps as 'Graves Plantation'. On modern maps this name refers to a strip of woodland but in the tithe map of 1847 this name refers to the wood now called 'Newton Gorse', while the strip is called 'Hides Drive'. Since 1847 the wood has become larger taking in a field formerly known as Little Graves (see Map 6). It is this larger wood that is still called Graves Plantation by local people, and is believed to be the site of one of the grave pits of the Battle of Shrewsbury. There are hedges near the plantation that date from a time either close to the battle or before it. One at the top of the hill above the plantation is probably at least 800 years old[4]. Can this be a site of a grave pit? If the battle took place closer to Harlescott, the answer must be that it is certainly possible. We can imagine a body of Hotspur's men, probably on foot, perhaps returning from plundering the King's baggage, attempting to avoid the main pursuit to the North making their way back to the ford at Berwick. Indeed if they were Welsh, this would be their best way home. Perhaps they were caught on the way and made a last stand at the top of the hill above the plantation, where they gave up their lives. However the graves, if they exist, may have nothing whatever to do with the battle. This is something that only archaeology can determine.

Two Oak trees

Perhaps because of their longevity many oaks are associated with events in English history. Some are associated with battles and have become known as "Battle Oaks". As far as any dating from battles in the middle ages are concerned these have now perished but we know where some of them stood, as for instance the Battle Oak at Mortimer's Cross which commemorated the battle of that name in 1461.

Oaks have now lost their former importance in English society and are reduced to being havens of wildlife or means to purer air. However for most of English history they were indispensable. They provided wood for building – houses, ships, carts, wheels, barrels, agricultural equipment, and fire wood; acorns for feeding stock, particularly pigs, bark for tanning and even the leaves were used. For this reason oak trees were planted, cared for and felled, mostly when they were between one hundred and two hundred years. Where they were coppiced they would have been felled much earlier. Nowadays we know of large numbers of relatively old oak trees: such trees were not evident in the past. They would have been cut down much sooner, put to good use and others planted or allowed to self sow. For this reason any oaks that were allowed to grow on in cultivated districts did so because they fulfilled some other purpose, perhaps as the marker for a boundary, to provide shade on the village green or to commemorate some event. There were two oaks which are believed to have some connection with the Battle of Shrewsbury.

The Shelton or Glyndwr's Oak.

This formerly stood close to the junction of the Oswestry and Welshpool roads at Shelton. It had an eventful history. At one time, after it was quite hollow inside, it became home for a performing bear! It was removed to make way for road improvements in 1950s. By that time it was long dead. In the 18th century a legend is reported that Owain Glyndwr sat in this tree to watch the Battle of Shrewsbury and, because of the strength of the King's forces, decided not to become involved and marched away. This legend has rightly been discounted by historians; Owain Glyndwr was at that time in South Wales. However, it is probable that the tree did indeed exist at the time of the battle because in 1543, the tenant at Shelton, one Adam Waring refers in a document to a 'grette oake' which stood on his land. Whether the oak had anything at all to do with the battle is unknowable, it would however have commanded the Silver Ford, so one can well imagine scouts from one side or the other using it as a vantage point. However it does provide perhaps a significant piece of negative evidence about the site of the Battle of Shrewsbury. Countless generations of small, (and large), boys and girls who climbed into the tree and had heard the story of Owain Glyndwr would have been able to see that the legend, if it referred to the site of the battle at Battlefield Church was impossible. For while Cross Hill, and indeed Harlescott crossroads are visible from Shelton, Battlefield Church is not. This means that the traditional site of the battle, as understood in the 17th, 18th and 19th centuries was not near to Battlefield Church.

Broad Oak

An immense oak tree used to stand close to the main road by the gate to Albright Hussey. This tree has given its name to the hamlet 'Broad Oak'. The tree has now virtually entirely disappeared (there is a small remnant of the stump still to be found in the front hedge of Oak Cottage). Most of its original site is now under the tarmac at the entrance to Albright

Hussey drive. There is a photograph of the tree dated 1897 and a watercolour dated 1891[5]. Both show a very large tree trunk indeed, but the branches have nearly all been blown down. Apparently one branch inflicted considerable damage to the roof of Oak Cottage behind it. At the turn of the 20th century some writers linked this tree to the battle, and there has even been a suggestion that it may mark the place where Hotspur was killed. It is impossible to know from the pictures how old it was in the 1890s but an age of more than 500 years would not be unreasonable. However, as it stood almost exactly on the parish boundary between Battlefield and Albrighton, it may have been a boundary oak rather than anything connected to the battle. This does not preclude the possibility that it was subsequently connected in local tradition with the battle. As will be explained below, it is not at all impossible that Hotspur's horses and baggage was stationed near this spot during the battle.

The site of Hotspur's death.
In his book, *The Battle of Shrewsbury 1403*, E.J. Priestley gives us this tantalising sentence: "A local newspaper report, of 18th September 1822, refers to a spot a mile to the west of Battlefield Church as the place traditionally identified as the site where Hotspur died." Of all the research I have undertaken on the battle this sentence remains the most tantalising. To what local paper does he refer? There is a Wellington Chronicle for this date, but it contains no such reference. The contemporary Salopian Journal also yields nothing. However the Salopian Journal for 25th September 1822 does contain the following *"At night, an immense bonfire was made opposite Mr Salter's at Battlefield near the spot where Hotspur is reported to have fallen..."* Whether this report is an any way connected to that reported by Priestley is not clear: but Priestley, a careful scholar, does place the traditional place for Hotspur's death a mile west of Battlefield. Perhaps he had discovered where Mr Salter lived. At that date properties in the hamlet of Broad Oak would have been considered as being in Battlefield as it was within Battlefield Parish. However we must be cautious about local traditions. They may be correct, but they may contain information that is entirely fabricated, so there needs to be some other very good reason to accept them as the truth.

Cross Hill
Many battle fields were commemorated by crosses erected near the site after the battle. For instance, the battle of Towton has a cross, as does

the battle of Wakefield. Probably many more battles had these crosses but like so many churchyard crosses, they became objects for destruction by iconoclastic forces of Oliver Cromwell.* Even the crosses at Towton and Wakefield suffered this destruction, Towton's was beheaded and Wakefield's is a nineteenth century replacement.

In the Middle Ages memorials to the dead were reserved exclusively for the upper classes who could afford elaborate tombs adorned with stone effigies, or when it became the fashion, brasses. Most people were commemorated by the church yard cross, which served as a memorial for all. It is not surprising that the dead from a battle were also commemorated by a cross often set up in a place where it was visible from a long distance. Sometimes these crosses were sited according to some other criteria, such as where someone particular was killed or where a commander was stationed. There is a prominent hill south of Harlescott crossroads dominating the main road (formerly 'Cross Lane') leading north from Shrewsbury, called Cross Hill. Was there once a cross on this hill, near where the farm now stands? Did this cross commemorate the fallen from the Battle of Shrewsbury? Just to the South of Cross Hill there is a farm lane leading to the west. This is the scene of a 'place imprint'† which might, perhaps, be associated with the battle. Several people have heard the sound of marching feet travelling along this lane towards Harlescott. While I would in no way suggest that this can be considered as historical evidence of any kind, it may whet the curiosity of some readers.

King's Croft

To the southeast of Battlefield Church is a field marked as King's Croft on the maps. It is notable for a medieval ridge-and-furrow field system. There are several fields with such features in the Battlefield and Albrighton area. It has been suggested that the name 'King's Croft' in some way connects this field with the battle. In 1903 an article appeared in the T.S.A.S. suggesting that the various mounds and depressions on the ground were witness to fortifications dug by the King's forces before the battle. No one has accepted that this is the case and for several reasons it seems unlikely. Shrewsbury itself belonged to the King, and as we have seen near to King's Croft was a royal college. It is probable that a field close by might belong to the King and be remembered as such. This might have been a place where forces of the King camped the night before the battle, or there may be some other connection.

The location of King's Croft presents a problem. It is marked on the Corbet estate survey map of 1777. However, the 1879 Ordnance Survey map places King's Croft in a different field, one that was formerly called 'Four Cornered Piece'. Another field today shown as 'King's Croft' was called Troopers Piece in 1777. The field originally called King's Croft has now virtually all disappeared under the railway and Shrewsbury by-pass. Troopers Piece, a miserable wet field, does show a ridge and furrow system, typical for the area, but a lot wider than the usual 'running rod' (five and a half yards) that was the normal medieval measure for a strip.

Documentary evidence

The important documents for locating the Battle of Shrewsbury are those written soon after the battle by those who had fought in it. The majority of such documents merely record that the battle was at Shrewsbury or was near Shrewsbury. Here is an example:

> *The King to Thomas de Portyngton ..and others etc. greeting. On behalf of Gerard Salvayn, it has been shown to us that although he was not in the company of Thomas Earl of Worcester, Henry Percy chivaler, and other rebels,* **in the battle near Salop against us,** *or as he says consented to the insurrection of the rebels, yet you have taken and carried off eleven oxen and 47 cows and other goods and chattels of the same Gerard to no small value, at Holm and Hertwell, in contempt of us and contrary to the form of our proclamation. We enjoin you to restore the oxen, cows and all other goods and chattels of the same Gerard to him without delay, etc. Witness the King at York the 11th day of August. (1403)[6]*

Such documents, however interesting, tell us nothing specific about the location of the battle. A number of other documents are, however, more specific and require closer scrutiny.

There is for instance the account of the Sheriff of Shropshire:

> *Salop. The Account of William Banastre, sheriff of Salop, of costs and expenses laid out and paid by him about the carriage of the four quarters of the body of Henry Percy and the head of baron Kynnerton, and the head of Richard Vernon chivaler, who lately made insurrection against the king and his royal majesty and against the debt of their allegiance* **at Husefeld near Salop** *on Saturday on the vigil of blessed Mary Magdalene…etc. (1403).[7]*

This gives us the local name of the battle very soon after the event from the most important King's officer in Shrewsbury - the sheriff himself. He used the name Husefeld i.e. Hussey Field. In November of 1403 the King himself uses this name.

Grant to our beloved Esquire Roger Acton of all the lands and tenements rents & services which belonged to John Russale esq. In cos Salop and York, forfeited to us, inasmuch as the same John against us and our faithful lieges fought with Henry Percy traitor & was killed in the **battle of Husifeld** ... *etc Witness the King at Westminster the 26th of November.[8]*

Another document, although rather later (1416) in the reign of Henry V is more specific, even though the field is spelt differently in two places. This document is of the greatest importance. It refers to evidence taken on oath before the escheator, a King's officer who was responsible for the escheats - that is land that has become, or might become, forfeit to the feudal lord or the crown for want of an heir. It refers to an enquiry into the affairs of Sir John Massy of Tatton:

Inquisition taken at Salop on Thursday next before the feast of the Purification of the Virgin Mary 3 Hen. V before William Hord eschetor, by oath of Richard Huse, Richard Stury, Robert Lee, John Lyise, John Lee, Richard Yonge, Robert Rodyngton, Guy Lowe, William Betton, Richard Browne, John Newbald and William Forster who say that John Massy of Tatton Chivaler died on Saturday in the vigil of St Mary Magdalene in the fourth year of Henry IV lately King of England, **at Bolefild in the town of Harlescote near Salop,** *having traitorously made insurrection with armed men, lances, banners unfurled &c., in a warlike manner against the aforesaid Henry lately King and his allegiance, with Henry Percy a rebel against the said King, in order to destroy annihilate and efface Henry IV King of England. And that the said John Massy,* **at the battle of Bolefeld in the town aforesaid,** *like a traitor and a rebel, fought with the aforesaid lord King with lances, standards unfurled &c. And in fighting with the King, the said John Massy was killed. And the said John Massy had no lands or tenements in my bailiwick, neither goods nor chattels.*
The Writ is dated 16th July 3 Henry V (1416).[9]

This document is very significant for the following reasons. First, it is intended to show that Sir John Massy **was** a rebel, ("lances, banners unfurled etc."); **when** he was a rebel ("Saturday in the vigil of St Mary Magdalene in the fourth year of Henry IV"); **why** he was a rebel ("with Henry Percy a rebel against the said King"), and then, for our purpose most important of all **where** he was a rebel ("at Bolefild in the town of Harlescote near Salop"). Second it is the testimony of twelve local Shropshire gentry sworn in Shrewsbury, with mention of the place of the battle - Bolefeld (perhaps bull field?) at Harlescott. It unquestionably refers to the battle because it mentions Hotspur (Henry Percy), and to the insurrection: with 'lances and banners'. The first to swear is Richard Huse, or Hussey who not only lived at Albright Hussey and himself fought at the battle, but it was **he who gave Hateley Field to Roger Ive for the foundation of Battlefield College**. If the battle took place at Hateley field, why did he not say so? But he and his eleven colleagues are quite adamant:. the battle took place at Bolefeld in Harlescott.

There can be only one conclusion. The battle was fought much closer to Harlescott itself than it was to Battlefield Church.

Archaeology

Several authors have raised the possibility that a number of artefacts connected with the battle might be found, which would give an indication of where the battle took place. One of the first was Charles Darwin who reported in 1881 of the discovery of a "surprising number of iron arrowheads ...in a grass field .. on the northern side of the Severn." But what does this mean? What is a surprisingly large number? Five? Fifty? Five hundred? And even if they were found, does that necessarily link them to the battle?

At the beginning of the fifteenth century any wrought iron was a very valuable commodity, especially armour and weapons. All the bodies of the fallen and badly wounded would have been stripped after the battle, and local people would have made it their business to recover everything in the way of clothing, weaponry or armour. No piece of iron would have been too small for a local blacksmith to turn into something useful[10]. Although some things were left on the battlefield, they would have been items that were lost - trampled into the ground, or arrows loosed into trees or undergrowth - hardly things to give any real indication as to the location of the battle. Even if rusting and ancient pieces of iron are found, are they really pieces of weaponry or equipment, or are they pieces of plough, hoe or cultivator sheared off against the many small boulders in these fields? Are they even broken items from the nineteenth century, thrown on to a farm midden and then distributed on the land.

The Battle of Shrewsbury was not the only military activity to take place in the area. During the Civil War a small royalist garrison was based in Albright Hussey, and on at least one occasion was attacked by parliamentarians from Wem. Items from this engagement may be wrongly attributed to the earlier battle. Even if, a couple of swords were found which could be dated to the early fifteenth century, what would they prove? The answer is no – they would not, they could have been lost in some quite different way, but one must acknowledge they would be an interesting pointer. No such finds have come to light. Arrow heads are even less of a guide: arrows could be lost while practising and while hunting, particularly in woodland.

Items that may be found on the battlefield that could be significant are brass buckles. These were used to join the leather straps that held on a suit of armour. Finding them exactly demonstrates our problem. Are they in a place because they were cut off in the battle, or because that was where some wounded soldiers crawled and then cut off their armour? Or were they where local peasants found dead men who had fled the battle, and there stripped them and cut off the armour?

Archaeology is best suited for human activity that has taken place over many centuries: where buildings have been raised and trenches and pits dug. Often, even after centuries of occupation, little may found in the way of artefacts. Therefore we should not expect to find very much from a battle that probably only lasted for a couple of hours. There is little point in investigating the battlefield itself, whether by digging or by metal detector. Such kind of investigation cannot really provide any useful information. However where there have been earthworks archaeology might help. It would be interesting to investigate the Graves Plantation, Cross Hill and underneath Battlefield Church.

---

* There is considerable irony in the fact that the puritans and their enthusiastic successors while rejecting the universal symbol of Christianity – the cross, were most happy to erect obelisks as commemorative monuments instead. Obelisks are, in origin, entirely pagan!

† A place imprint is phenomena that should be described as natural that is as yet unexplained. The effect is that people see, or hear, some event that took place at some time in the past, like a phantom coach careering round a bend. They are often associated either with some frequently repeated action, or some drama. For some unknown reason this event is visible or audible to people when the correct circumstances are in operation. They are not necessarily associated with death, indeed there are people who have seen place imprints of themselves.

Many are I believe so commonplace that we do not even notice them at all. I myself witnessed a phantom cyclist, hundreds of times, on my journey home some years ago, and evidently other motorists did as well as they indicated to pass him. He then just disappeared! For more on this see: *But deliver us from Evil* by John Richards

[1] Patent 8 Henry IV, pars 1 mem. 28. In T.S.A.S series 3 vol. 3 p. 179

[2] See T.S.A.S series 3 vol. 3 p. 177 ff

[3] Harlein MS 566, Cottonian MS Julius B1

[4] For an introduction to dating hedges see *Hedges* by E. Pollard, M.D. Hooper and N.W. Moore. The system depends on the number of hedge species in a given length of hedge. This system has to be treated with considerable caution as a hedge could be planted with more than one species and nowadays often are. I am however reasonably confident with the dating given.

[5] Shropshire Records 6001/225. Some of the last vestigial remains of the stump the 'Broad Oak' are still present in the front hedge of Oak Cottage.

[6] T.S.A.S Vol. XII 1900 p.42

[7] T.S.A.S Vol. X 1898 p.243

[8] T.S.A.S. Vol. III series 3 1903

[9] T.S.A.S. Vol. X 1898 p.249 ff

[10] An indication of the significance of iron can be had from the Chronicle of Lanercost Priory account of the 'Great Raid' when the Scottish King, Robert the Bruce, invaded North-west England in 1322 burning, murdering and looting as he went. Lancaster, Cartmel, Ulverston and many other places suffered. The Chronicle states "They seized all the manufactured iron that they could find and carried it off with the greatest joy, although so heavy of carriage and preferred it to other plunder" mentioned in *Furness Abbey* by Alice Leach

The Monument which marks the site of the Shelton Oak.

Chapter 5

Where was the battlefield?
Identifying the site

Where was the Battle of Shrewsbury fought?

Although it would be good to be able to say with absolute certainty where the forces of Hotspur and Henry IV were drawn up on that July morning of 1403, the best that can now be done is to give a broad idea of where they were, because so much has changed, some of it extremely recently. First of all, however, it is necessary to establish why the battle could not have been in the Battlefield Church area. This site must now be abandoned for the following reasons:

1) *Battlefield Church as a grave pit.*
As we have seen above, although the church, or its churchyard, may well be the site of a grave pit, this does not therefore prove that it was the site of the centre of the battle, or even close to it. Furthermore, it is very probable that it was not the only grave pit associated with the battle, at least one other being at Graves Plantation.

2) *The sworn evidence of Richard Hussey places the battle elsewhere.*
Although in the charters establishing the College at Battlefield it is referred to, *perhaps*, as being the site of the battle, the sworn testimony of the founder of the college, Richard Hussey, along with eleven other local men, placing the field of battle at a different site should convince the most partisan supporter of the Battlefield Church site that this belief is unsound.

3) *The site of the battle must make strategic or military sense to the commanders.*
The position that Hotspur chose for the battle must have related to the military position he found himself in. If he lost the battle, he needed to leave the field in reasonable order and subsequently join up with his father to continue the struggle. Hotspur cannot have left his line of retreat unguarded. Hotspur received reinforcements along the Chester Road, i.e. from Myddle via Albrighton, along what is now the A528

Ellesmere road. It is probable that he himself approached Shrewsbury along this road having travelled through Wem from Whitchurch and Prees. It is reasonable that securing this route would be his first priority, as it allowed a withdrawal either on Chester or Wem and Whitchurch. It is most unlikely that he would have left this retreat uncovered, yet this is precisely what a position near to Battlefield Church would have done. If Hotspur took up a position north of Battlefield Church, even a small force belonging to the King, could have marched straight up the road, outflanked Hotspur and secured the road against his retreat.

It could be argued that a position north of Battlefield Church covered the Whitchurch road, what we now call the A49. However, this was neither the main road in 1403, nor a particularly fast one, and there is no evidence that Hotspur's forces used it. Furthermore the position which most modern authors assign to Hotspur is well west of the church, in which case his position does not cover the Whitchurch road either.

However, some consideration needs to be given to Wheets Lane. This is a lane or drover's road, that originally ran from Harlescott, past the site of Battlefield Church (it goes through the vicarage garden) and then on to Hadnall. It can now only be traced by the hedges that originally bordered it; some of these have been recently replanted. Because a footpath runs from the lane to Battlefield, I had assumed that it owed its existence to Battlefield College and was to be dated after the battle. However, I believe that this may be unsound, for three reasons. The first is that it does not actually go to Battlefield Church, but past it. Second, it is used as a parish boundary for much of its length. Third, there are at least two sections of hedge which originally bordered the lane that are of great antiquity, perhaps seven or eight hundred years old. It is safer to conclude that the College is placed where it is because of Wheets Lane, rather than the other way round. It was used, I believe, by Hotspur's forces to flee the battle, and for carts to take bodies from the battle to the church site.

4) *King Henry IV was much closer to Battlefield Church than Hotspur.* We know that on the morning of the battle Hotspur was himself at Berwick. We may conclude that his forces were either concentrated at Berwick guarding the Silver Ford, or before the Castle Gate of Shrewsbury itself. The King with probably the bulk of his army was concentrated somewhere close to Uffington and Haughmond. Thus the King was actually *closer* by more than a mile to Battlefield Church than Hotspur! (see Map 2) If, then, the battle took place where it is generally placed – close to Battlefield Church – we are expected to imagine the King allowing Hotspur to march across his front in order to take up his battle

position! This is most improbable. Whatever other military attributes we may ascribe to Henry IV, lethargy is certainly not one of them. He acted with remarkable promptness, rushing all available forces to Shrewsbury as fast as he could. On 20th July he had Hotspur potentially pinned against the river in a most unfavourable position, with his line of retreat cut off. It is unlikely that he would now allow Hotspur to march across his front in order to take up a position to his (the King's) disadvantage.

5) *Hotspur did not place his forces in woodland.*

The actual position ascribed by authors to Hotspur do not in fact bear scrutiny. The area to the north of a line drawn between Albright Hussey and Battlefield Church – now a lane – was probably not fully in cultivation in the 18th century, let alone the 15th. From the names of some of the fields in 1777, it is clear that they were only recently either wood or uncultivated heath land. For instance some are called 'Little Hurst', and 'Big Hurst', (Hurst from the Old English meaning a wood or grove); others are called names like 'Meesons Gorst', and 'Gamstons Gorst', (Gorst from the Old English meaning Gorse i.e. heath land). Hotspur drew up his forces in a broad field that was in cultivation not in woodland! If the battle did take place in this area, the most advantageous position would be approximately along the line of the lane between the church and Albright Hussey. To the north there is dead ground, kettle holes and clay pits, which would not be to Hotspur's advantage at all.

6) *There are some other minor reasons.*

The traditions about the oak trees, the Graves Plantation, the site of Hotspur's death, cannot be made to fit in with siting the battle near Battlefield Church.[†] Something should also be said about Featherbed Lane. It is said that the wounded from the battle were taken here after the battle. As it is directly to the rear of the King's position, this seems quite likely. Perhaps it is so named through a piece of English military irony! These are conclusive in themselves, but taken with the other factors lead to one conclusion: the Battle of Shrewsbury was not fought around Battlefield Church.

[†] The only other feature, apart from the church itself, that *could* be connected with the Battlefield area is King's Croft. However, in light of all the other evidence my conclusion is that *if* this is indeed something to do with the battle it refers to the night before the battle rather than to the battle itself. It is certainly much too tenuous a piece of evidence to make any difference whatever to the main conclusion: The Battle of Shrewsbury was not centred around Battlefield Church.

'Cross Lane' from the south – the 'narrow pass'?

Conclusion

Where, then, was the Battlefield?

If the Battle of Shrewsbury was not fought around Battlefield Church where was it fought? The starting point must be the oath of Richard Hussey. It was at Bolefeld in Harlescott. A site somewhere near Harlescott makes perfect sense. If the King was moving his forces to overtake Hotspur and cut his retreat, he would move along the most direct route from the Uffington - Haughmond area to the main Chester road. This would take him along what are now called the picturesquely sounding Featherbed Lane and more prosaic Harlescott Lane. Likewise Hotspur, moving to protect his retreat, would march straight north up the Chester road. Assuming they travelled at the same speed and started at the same moment, they would arrive at the Harlescott crossroads at almost exactly the same time. Of course we cannot assume either of these things. It is probable that Hotspur, whose need was greatest, arrived first. He chose farmland, but it does not seem to me that the phrase, *"They chose, as it seemed, the more advantageous ground, as the King's army, should it wish to engage, would have to advance across a broad field thickly sown with pease"* implies that there was very much advantage to Hotspur from the point of view of height. He may have positioned his forces on the highest ground he could find in order to give his archers some advantage.

However, although I do not accept that the battle was fought in the area around Battlefield Church, neither do I accept that it was fought very far away from it. It was certainly close enough for men to run to that area after the battle. There is no reason to believe that the King had actually cut off Hotspur's line of retreat and had forced him to take up a position with his back to the river. If this had happened, there would have been no chance of Hotspur being reinforced, which we are told was a possibility. Reports of the battle would also have mentioned such a major military advantage to the King.

The village of Harlescott is not mentioned in accounts of the battle. We are not told of houses or the moat that may have already have been dug[1].

We must look for the site of the Battle of Shrewsbury somewhere between the hamlets of Broad Oak and Harlescott. There are two possibilities either a position north of the present by-pass with Hotspur's right wing close to the road with his line stretching in a roughly northeast/southwest direction, or a position slightly south of the present by-pass and further to the east – see Map 7. On balance I prefer the former but this may be coloured in my mind by the fact that most of it is still farmland while the southern site has disappeared under roads and industrial buildings. Nevertheless there is just enough, at the time of writing (2003), to be able to draw a reasonable conclusion where the battle would have been.

It would be good to be able to identify a Bolefeld in this area. Sadly none is to be found. There are extensive records of the names of fields in the area which are based on Tithe Maps, dating from either the 1770s or from the 1850s, by which time virtually all the area had been enclosed. There are far more fields shown on these maps than there would have been in 1403, and more field names. There are no Bole or Bull Fields. There are however a number of fields that are named after individuals, for instance 'Corbets Piece'. This frequently means that the field did not belong to the owner of the rest of the manor but to someone else. In Harlescott there is shown a 'Husseys Yard' – see Map 5. 'Yard' here means an enclosed field, usually attached to a house. From the map it would seem possible that this field was once much larger. Was it the site of the battle? It is not called Bull Field. But could it be that Hussey himself, because he owned the field, did not refer to it as 'Hussey Field' but as 'Bull Field'? This is over ingenious speculation. I am sure however that this field is close to the actual site of the battle.

What then of the *narrow pass*?
If the battle took place at Harlescott, there are at least two potential narrow passes. The one is the piece of road, known as "Cross Lane" i.e. where the main Chester road penetrates the escarpment of the Old Riverbed, or it could be the stream bed that leads to Hencott Pool. If there was an outflanking movement either could have provided cover. Sadly, we do not now know. There is, however, something that may provide enlightenment. If we accept the account of Jean de Breuil, we may ask the question how was it that the King managed to preserve a sufficiently fresh reserve to counter-attack Hotspur, overcome his reserve and then go on to win the battle? Perhaps it happened thus:

The King may have left a garrison at Shrewsbury when he marched to Uffington, the purpose of which was to stop Hotspur entering the town in the King's rear and also to make a sufficient demonstration to encourage Hotspur to stay close to Shrewsbury, allowing the King's main force time to cut Hotspur's retreat. This stratagem may have been successful, because Hotspur was evidently taken by surprise. At some point after Hotspur's army had left the immediate environs of Shrewsbury, this garrison would have been available to rejoin the King. When this happened would depend on the speed of Hotspur's rearguard, the speed with which orders were received from the King, and whether there was any kind of 'Welsh threat'. It is reasonable to suppose therefore that the garrison would not have moved until well after the King was in position, and would have travelled north along Cross Lane. They may have arrived just in time after battle was joined, and here may be the explanation of the 'narrow pass'.

[1] The moat at Harlescott still exists as a piece of litter strewn waste ground in the middle of some local authority housing at the back of the Anchor Inn.

Map 1

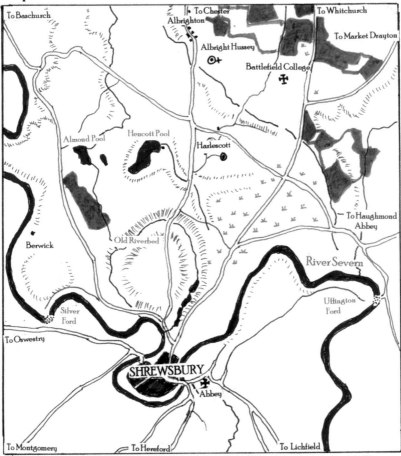

The area North of Shrewsbury in 1403 based on Ordnance Survey map 1833

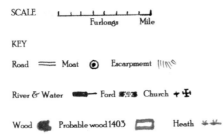

SCALE

Furlongs   Mile

KEY

Road ═══ Moat ◉ Escarpmemt ｜｜ｍ

River & Water ■■■━ Ford ⋙ Church ✝ ☦

Wood ◖ Probable wood 1403 ▭ Heath ⚘ ⚘

Map 1

The area north of Shrewsbury in 1403 based on the Ordnance Survey map 1833

The geography of Shrewsbury is dominated by the River Severn which is impassable except by bridge at Shrewsbury itself (there were two bridges in medieval times) and by ford, the Uffington Ford to the east and the Silver or Shelton Ford to the west.

The land to the north of Shrewsbury is undulating and rises gradually to about 300 feet at Albrighton. The 'Old Riverbed' is significant from a military point of view, as it confines the passage in to or out of Shrewsbury to a narrow strip of rising land sandwiched between the Old Riverbed and the Severn itself. In medieval times there were fishponds at this point, which would have accentuated this. The Old Riverbed is crossed by the Chester highway at one place, and skirted to the south by the road to Baschurch.

It is difficult to know how much land north of Shrewsbury was cultivated in 1403. Certainly there were two manors – at Albrighton held by Shrewsbury Abbey and at Albright Hussey (which included Harlescott) held by Richard Hussey. The year 1403 was only a couple of generations from the Black Death when a great deal of land, especially in the Midlands, went out of cultivation because so many people had died in the epidemic. We do not know what, if any, effect this may have had around Shrewsbury, but it is reasonable to assume that some land had reverted to waste. The amount of heath and waste land was probably greater than that shown on the map: for instance, there is reason to believe that there was more heath to the west of Harlescott. The area north of a line drawn from Battlefield College to Albright Hussey was probably mostly heath or woodland; to this day it is rather poor ground.

There may also have been woodland stretching from Uffington round to Albrighton. Hencott Pool, which has now virtually dried up to become a piece of woodland, was in medieval times a source of fish and water power. There was a monastic mill there.

The main route to Chester and the North was the direct route through Albrighton, what is now called the "Ellesmere Road", though, close to Shrewsbury, it is significantly still called "Chester Street". This was still the stagecoach route in the 18th and early 19th centuries. It is not the obvious route one would now use to travel between Shrewsbury and Chester.

N.B. In all the maps North is at the top of the page

Map 2

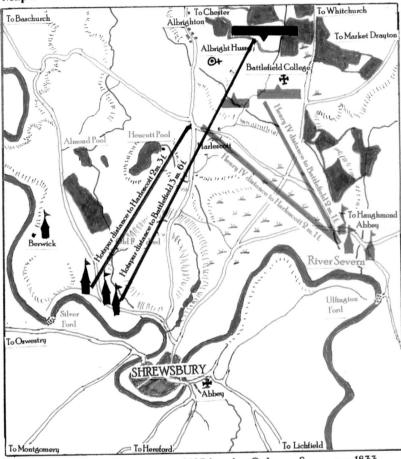

The area North of Shrewsbury in 1403 based on Ordnance Survey map 1833

SCALE

Furlongs   Mile

KEY

Road ═══ Moat ◉ Escarpment ⑂⑂⑂

River & Water ▰▰▰ Ford ▰▰▰ Church ✝ ✠

Wood ▰ Probable wood 1403 ▭ Heath ⩊ ⩊

Map 2

The distances the armies of Henry IV and Hotspur had to travel by road to arrive at a) the Battlefield Church area and b) Harlescott

The purpose of this map is to show the relative distance the two armies had to travel to reach the battlefield on the morning of 21st July.

The position that it traditionally considered to be the site of the battle may be seen to the north and south of Battlefield College. This position varies somewhat from author to author, but the position as shown is that adopted by the authors of the book *Two Men in a Trench* which accompanied the recent (2002) television series.

It will be seen that in order to arrive at the position shown, Hotspur's forces would have had to march about a mile and a half further than those of Henry IV. Although it is possible that they rose earlier and that Henry IV did nothing to stop them, this seems highly unlikely.

However, securing the cross roads at Harlescott would have been both an important strategic objective for Hotspur, and attainable without interference by the King.

Map 3

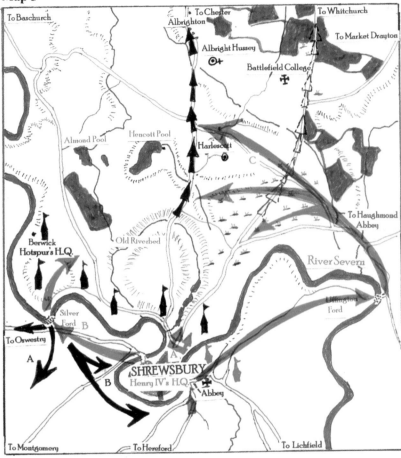

July 20th 1403 - The Strategical problems facing Henry IV (in red) and Hotspur (in black)

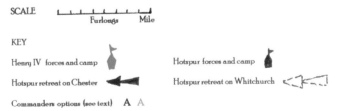

Map 3

July 20th 1403 – The strategical problems facing Henry IV (in red) and Hotspur (in black).

Henry IV: Having already secured Shrewsbury the problem for Henry IV was to bring Hotspur to battle as quickly as possible on the most favourable terms. He was faced with three options:-

A. march north attacking Hotspur's army outside the castle gate. This would have involved attacking uphill on a very narrow front, confined by the Old River Bed and the Severn. This would be a very unattractive proposition;

B. march west confronting Hotspur's army at the Silver Ford at Shelton. This option would be as unattractive as **A**;

C. march east north-east crossing the river at Uffington and then swing round to the west, cutting Hotspur's communications with the North and driving him back against the Severn. This is a much more attractive plan. For its best success, however, some kind of demonstration engaging Hotspur's attention close to Shrewsbury and the Silver Ford would probably be necessary. There is no evidence that such a demonstration took place, except that dawn on July 21st found Hotspur still at Berwick and Henry IV, with half his manoeuvre completed, close to Uffington and Haughmond.

Hotspur: Failing to take Shrewsbury on first arrival, it is reasonable to suppose that Hotspur sent at least some forces across the Severn to Shelton. This would have been necessary if he were to lay siege to the town. He could have decided either:

A. to continue his march south-west to join the Welsh or ...

B. continue south marching on Hereford.
In fact, neither would have been a serious consideration once he discovered the size of the force opposing him. This may not have been realised until quite late on the 20th July or even very early on the 21st, the day of the battle itself.

Thus the over-riding problem was to secure his retreat, allowing him to fall back on Chester or Whitchurch, and thus allowing the possibility of joining forces with his father, the Earl of Northumberland, in the North.

Map 4

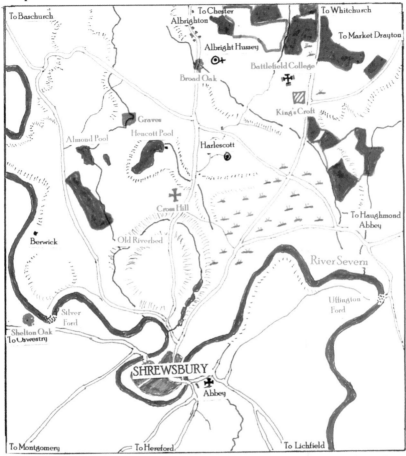

Features associated, or possibly associated, with the Battle of Shrewsbury (in red)

SCALE

Furlongs   Mile

KEY

Road   Moat   Escarpmemt

River & Water   Ford   Church

Wood   Probable wood 1403   Heath

Map 4

Features associated, or possibly associated, with the Battle of Shrewsbury (in red)

There are six features that have at one time been associated with the Battle of Shrewsbury:

Battlefield College. This was certainly founded as a result of the battle. The church is still in existence, as are the fish ponds in the old college grounds.

King's Croft. This is a field to the south east of Battlefield Church, which exhibits an extensive system of ridge and furrow strips.

Broad Oak. This no longer exists, but it stood close to the entrance to the drive leading to Albright Hussey

Graves. An area of woodland which has been variously described – Graves Plantation, Near Graves, Far Graves etc. This feature may be site of one of the grave pits from the battle; certainly this is the local belief. There are several hedges of considerable antiquity close to this site, and they may either have existed at the time of the battle or been planted soon after.

Cross Hill. A cross probably stood on this hill. It may have been connected with the battle.

Shelton Oak. A local tradition associates this tree with the battle. It no longer exists, but is commemorated by a monument that now stands on the site.

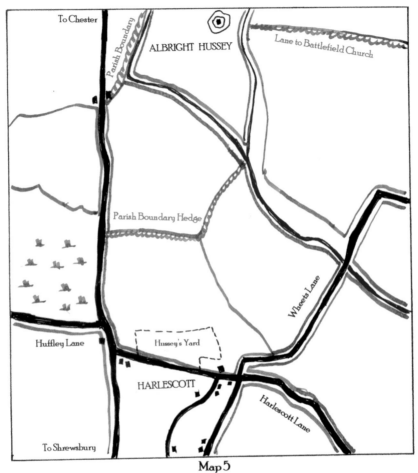

Map 5
The Location of Hussey's Yard
This plan is based on the field name maps in Shropshire Records and Research. These are drawn from Tithe maps of various dates. This is a composite map drawn from the Corbet Survey of 1777, the Albrighton Chapelry (Shrewsbury St Mary's) 1845, and Harlescott township (St Alkmund and St Mary Shrewsbury) 1849. The Green lines mark the possible extent of the 15th Century fields.

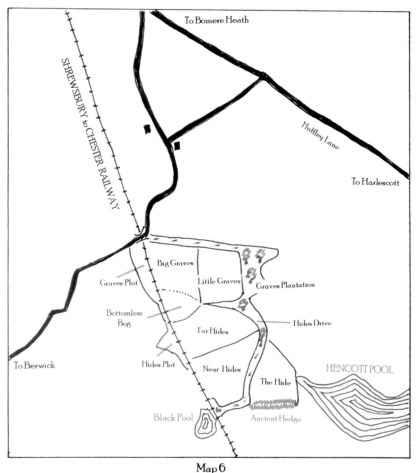

Map 6
The Location of the Graves

This plan is based on the field name maps in Shropshire Records and
Research. These are drawn from Tithe maps of various dates. This is a
composite map drawn from the Tithe Map of Hencott Grange (St Alkmund
Shrewsbury), and St Mary's (Shrewsbury), 1849. Notice that some of the fields
have been bisected by the building of the railway.

Map 7

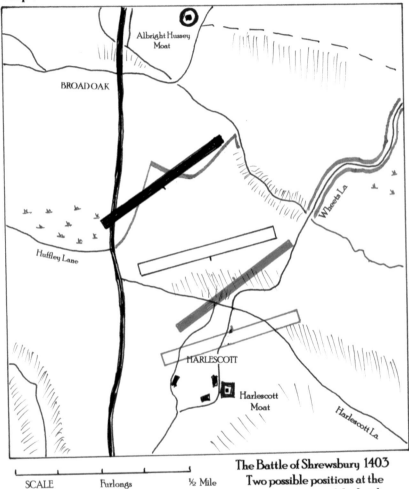

The Battle of Shrewsbury 1403
Two possible positions at the
commencement of the battle

SCALE   Furlongs   ½ Mile

KEY

Road ▬▬   Lane ——   Lane probably post 1403 – –   Hedge (1403) ▬▬

Heath ⅄   Stream ▬▬   Slope \\\

Hotspur's Army position 1 ▰▰   Hotspur's Army position 2 ▭

Henry IV's Army position 1 ▨▨   Henry IV's Army position 2 ▭

Map 7

The Battle of Shrewsbury 1403. Two possible positions at the commencement of the battle

There are two reasonable positions that Hotspur could have decided to give battle at Harlescott. They are close to each other and the course of the battle as described could have unfolded in the same way in either location. On balance the more northerly position seems preferable. However the ground and levels have recently been much disturbed by building the Shrewsbury By-pass and the Battlefield industrial estate. There is for instance now an area of standing water on the site which was not present even in 1998.

Map 8

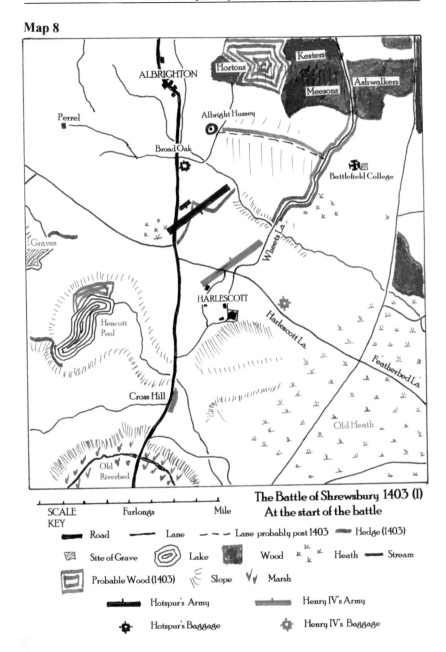

The Battle of Shrewsbury 1403 (I)
At the start of the battle

SCALE
KEY

Furlongs · Mile

Road — Lane — – – Lane probably post 1403 — Hedge (1403)

Site of Grave — Lake — Wood — Heath — Stream

Probable Wood (1403) — Slope — Marsh

Hotspur's Army — Henry IV's Army

Hotspur's Baggage — Henry IV's Baggage

Map 8

The Battle of Shrewsbury 1403 (I)

A suggested reconstruction of the battle based on the Annales and the account of Jean de Breuil and other records.

Hotspur marshals his forces to the northwest of "Bolefeld" with a mixed force of men-at-arms and archers in the centre, with archers on his wings. He keeps a small reserve of men-at-arms at the rear.

Henry IV marshals his forces in a similar fashion, with fewer archers but more men-at-arms.

The baggage of both armies is to the rear. This is where the horses would have been placed. The garrison from Shrewsbury are making their way to the battle up the Chester highway.

Note There was probably a hedge either side of Wheets Lane. The other hedges marked appear to be ancient. In the fifteenth century the countryside would have been more open than it is today, though there would have been considerably more woodland.

Map 9

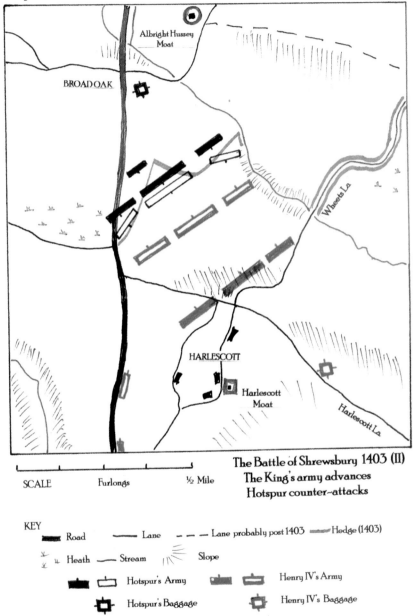

The Battle of Shrewsbury 1403 (II)
The King's army advances
Hotspur counter-attacks

SCALE   Furlongs   ½ Mile

KEY

Road   Lane   Lane probably post 1403   Hedge (1403)

Heath   Stream   Slope

Hotspur's Army   Henry IV's Army

Hotspur's Baggage   Henry IV's Baggage

Map 9

The Battle of Shrewsbury 1403 (II)

After the battle commences, the King's forces advance into the late afternoon sun. Hotspur's army advances to meet them, loosing a devastating hail of arrows. His wings advance, enfilading the King's forces. The garrison from Shrewsbury quickens its pace.

Map 10

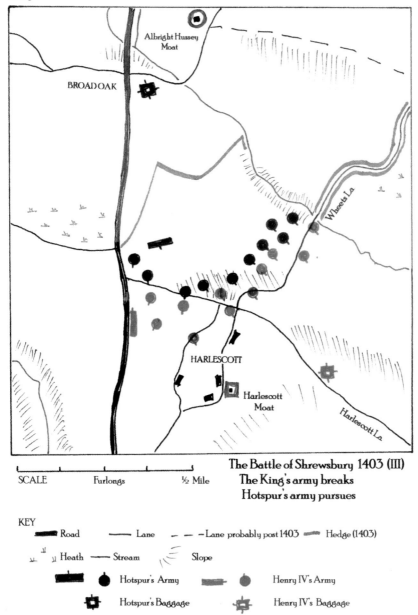

Albright Hussey
Moat

BROAD OAK

Wheets La

HARLESCOTT

Harlescott
Moat

Harlescott La

The Battle of Shrewsbury 1403 (III)
The King's army breaks
Hotspur's army pursues

SCALE   Furlongs   ½ Mile

KEY

━━ Road   ── Lane   ─ ─ ─ Lane probably post 1403   ━ ━ Hedge (1403)

Heath   ── Stream   Slope

━━ ● Hotspur's Army   ━━ ● Henry IV's Army

Hotspur's Baggage   Henry IV's Baggage

Map 10

The Battle of Shrewsbury 1403 (III)

The disciplined shooting of Hotspur's Cheshire bowmen is too much for the King's forces. They falter, and then turn and run. Many are shot as they flee.

On the King's left wing, however, the garrison of Shrewsbury has finally arrived. Prince Henry puts himself at their head, rallies what he can of his broken forces, and charges towards Hotspur and his reserve.

The King takes refuge with the garrison.

Map 11

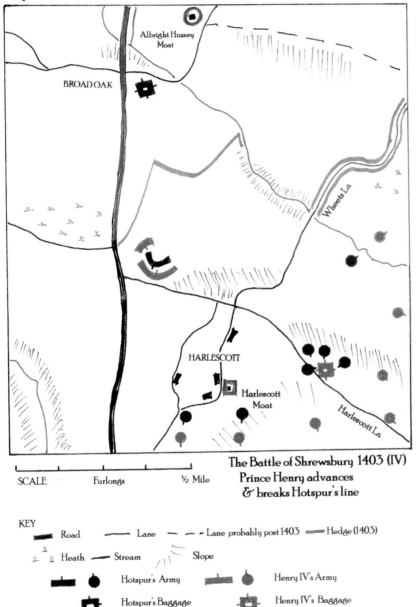

The Battle of Shrewsbury 1403 (IV)
Prince Henry advances
& breaks Hotspur's line

SCALE   Furlongs   ½ Mile

KEY

Road   Lane   — — Lane probably post 1403   Hedge (1403)

Heath   Stream   Slope

Hotspur's Army   Henry IV's Army

Hotspur's Baggage   Henry IV's Baggage

Map 11

The Battle of Shrewsbury 1403 (IV)

Most of the King's forces continue to flee from the field. Here and there they are pursued by Hotspur's men but the King's baggage is too big a prize for most of them. They abandon the pursuit, and loot the King's possessions and horses.

Meanwhile back on the battlefield, Hotspur finds his reserve surrounded by overwhelming forces, the garrison from Shrewsbury and what has been rallied of Prince Henry's left wing.

Map 12

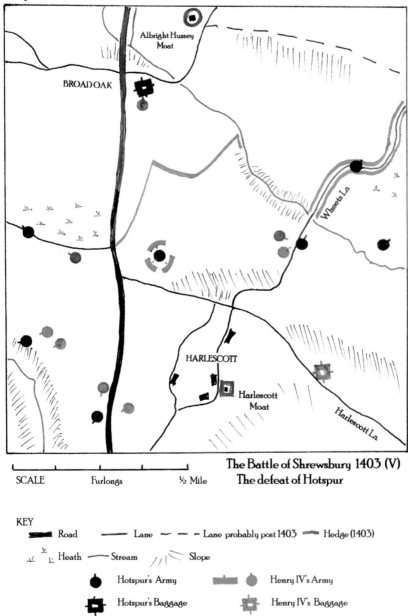

SCALE   Furlongs   ½ Mile

The Battle of Shrewsbury 1403 (V)
The defeat of Hotspur

KEY

▬▬ Road   —— Lane   — — – Lane probably post 1403   ▬▬ Hedge (1403)

Heath   —— Stream   ⁄⁄⁄ Slope

● Hotspur's Army   ▬● Henry IV's Army

⬛ Hotspur's Baggage   ⬛ Henry IV's Baggage

Map 12

The Battle of Shrewsbury 1403 (V)

The tables are now turned. Hotspur finds himself surrounded. With many of his followers he dies, others are captured, to face execution in two days. The King quickly mobilises the forces he has left and pursues the remains of Hotspur's army in several directions. Some flee westwards; others flee northeast. Those who have stolen a horse make good their escape; others are less fortunate. Meanwhile, many of the King's routed soldiers arrive at Shrewsbury Castle with the news that the day is lost and the King slain.